AMERICAN COLONISTS
IN
ENGLISH RECORDS

A Guide to direct references in authentic records, Passenger Lists not in "Hotten," &c., &c., &c.

By
GEORGE SHERWOOD

FIRST AND SECOND SERIES
Two Volumes in One

CLEARFIELD

Originally published: London, England
First Series, 1932
Second Series, 1933

Reprinted, two volumes in one, by
Genealogical Publishing Co., Inc.
Baltimore, Maryland
1961, 1969, 1978, 1982

Library of Congress Catalogue Card Number 63-518

Reprinted for Clearfield Company by
Genealogical Publishing Company
Baltimore, Maryland
2011

ISBN 978-0-8063-0310-9

Made in the United States of America

PREFATORY NOTE

DIRECT references in English records to colonists in New England and America are extraordinarily hard to come by. Hundreds of pounds are spent annually in searching for them. The following are presented as the result of constant daily search covering the last forty years, and they will be useful, it is hoped, in this form for reference. A healthy sale of the book will enable the compiler to give his whole time to the search for these "missing links." A good thing, surely, for here we strike the note of Anglo-American kinship and the consolidation of all that is best in the English-speaking world.

G. S.

In the Principal Probate Registry, London.

P.C.C. 71 WOOD.

609, April 23.

SOMERS, Sir George, of Barne, Dorset, Knight, "intending to voyage to Virginia," his will names John, William and Tobie, sons, and Mary, daughter of John, my brother, and others, but none in Virginia.

In the Principal Probate Registry, London.

P.C.C. 77 CAPELL.

609, May 5.

ATKINSON, William, the younger of London, gent., bound to Virginia, his will names William A., of London, Esquire, "my father," Thomas A., of Penrith, Cumberland, and Raphe A., of Woborne Dayncourte, Bucks, gentleman, executors.

In the Principal Probate Registry, London.

P.C.C. 35 WOOD.

609, June 1.

SICKLEMORE *alias* RATCLIFFE, John, captain of "The Diamond," bound for Virginia, his will names his wife Dorothie.

PERCIVALL, Richard, Esq., "my lovinge freinde," executor.

In the Principal Probate Registry, London.

P.C.C. 66 COPE.

1609, Sept. 7.

ANDREWS, John, of Cambridge, co. Cambridge, merchaunt, "intending to go into Ireland," in his will names his wife Easter, sons John, William, Francis, Richard and George, daughters Easter, Elizabeth and Sara. "My stock with the Virginia Company."
Codicil, 22 March, 1610, "Death of my sonne John ANDREWS in Virginea."

In the Principal Probate Registry, London.

P.C.C. 60 COPE.

A.D.

1610. WEST, William, of Dedsham in Slinfold, Sussex, gent., "then taking his voyage into Virginea where he dyed," made his will nuncupative naming—
BLUNT, Mary, wife of Richard of Dedsham, Esquire, universal legatee.

In the Principal Probate Registry, London.

P.C.C. 15 FENNER.

1611, May 10.

BENNINGTON, Richard, carpenter of "The Unicorne," bound to Vergeina, his will names
ARNOLD, Robert, my friend, sole executor.

In the Principal Probate Registry, London.

P.C.C. 85 CAPEL.

1612, Nov. 9.

NELSON, Francis, of the precinct of St. Katherine's, London, mariner, in his will mentions his voyages to Virginia and for discovery of the North West Passage.
NELSON, *alias*
HANDLEY, Annie, my mother, now dwelling in Sadbery, co. York.
NELSON, Elizabeth, and
SHERWOOD, Anne, my sisters, and
NELSON, Daniel, my cousin.

In the Principal Probate Registry, London.

P.C.C. 105 RUDD.

1615, Oct. 24.

ANTHONYE, Charles, of S^t. John Zachary, London, "cheife graver of the Kyng's Ma^{ts} Mynt and of his Seales, his will names his wife Elizabeth, his children Thomas, Richard, Charles, James, Andrew, Edward and Marye, my brother Francis A. "My one hundred and ten pounds adventure into the Sommer Ilandes, and £137 adventure into the first Colonye into Virginia."
ARNOLD, Samuel, my brother in law, to be overseer.

In the Principal Probate Registry, London.

P.C.C. 19 DALE.

1617, Dec. 19.
SMALLAY, Captain Robert, "of the Bermoda hundred," in his will names his wife Elizabeth.
HARDYN, Christopher, my man.
CHAPMAN, Thomas, my man.
KYES, Richard, my man.
OGE, Thomas, my man.
PEERS, M^r.
CHAPLYN, Ensigne.
PROCTER, M^r.
BARTLET, Leivetent.
DALE, Sir Thomas.
ARGALL, Capt. Samuel, Esq., now Governor of Virginea, executor.
RICHARDSON, Henry, and
DOWNEMAN, John, witnesses.

Records of the Drapers' Company, London.

A.D.
1620/21. £3 is paid "Appellinge of CHESWRIGHTE to be sent to Virginia." Richard CHESEWRIGHT made free of the Company 23 Jan. 1597 by Richard OSBORNE. In 1612 mentioned in Richard OSBORNE's will.

In the Principal Probate Registry, London.

P.C.C. 49 SCROOPE.

1621, March 10.
ROLFFE, John, of James Cittie in Virginia, Esquire, his will names his "two small children of very tender age."
PYERS, Lievetennant William, gent., my father in lawe. My land in the county of Toppahanna between the two creeks over against James Cittie. My son Thomas, Elizabeth my daughter. My land near Mulberie Iland, Virginia, to Joane my wife.
DAVIES, Robert, my servant.
YEARDLEY, Temperance.
BUCK, Richard.
CARTWRIGHT, John, and
MILWARDE, John, witnesses.
Proved at London 21 May, 1630, by William PYERS.

In the Principal Probate Registry, London.

P.C.C. 55 BARRINGTON.

1622, Sept. 10. At Elizabeth Citty in Virginia.
WILLCOCKS, Captain John, late of Plimouth and now of Ackamack in Virginia "intending to transporte myselfe for a piece of service against and upon the Indians," his will names "my wife Temperance, my sisters Katherin and Susana W."
BURGES, Grace, "my daughter in lawe and legitimate daughter to my said wife Temperance."
NUSE, Captain Thomas, and
PONTIS, John, to be overseers.
STOCKTON, James, and
ARONDELL, P., witnesses.
Proved at London 11 June, 1628, by Temperance, the relict, who was sworn before Henry WALLIS, vicar of Plymouth.

In the Principal Probate Registry, London.

P.C.C. 78 BYRDE.

A.D.

1624. DOMBLAWE, Richard, of London, bachelor, in his will entreats
MATHEWES, Captain, and
FARRAR, Mʳ William, " to take into their handes all such goodes as belongeth to me in Virginia and to pay all my debtes in Virginia." Estate in England to be divided between my brothers and sisters and one
BARNES, Mathewe.
(Signs " DOMELAW.")
WEST, Fras.,
HOLMES, William, and
BARNES, MATHEWE, are witnesses.
No date, but administration 9 Sept. 1624, to
DOMELAW, John, S.T.B.,
the brother.

In the Principal Probate Registry, London.

P.C.C. 106 HELE.

1625, Sept. 10.
BIGGS, Richard, of West and Sherley hundreds, Virginia, his will names his wife Sara and son Richard.
SHARPE, Samuell, my lovinge frende.
ROSE, Rebecka, my sister.
WOODWARDE, Christopher, his grounde by the Swampe side.
PAWLETT, Thomas, and Samuell SHARPE witnesses.
Administration 9 Aug. 1626, to Sara the relict.

In the Principal Probate Registry, London.

P.C.C. 33 SEAGER.

625, Dec. 17.
WEST, Francis, of Winchester, co. Southampton, Esq., in his will names Jane, my now wife, dau. of Sir Henry DAVYE, Knt. My plantations, &c., in Virginia; son Francis under 21. Proved at London 28 April, 1634, by Jane, the relict.

Records of the Drapers' Company, London.

A.D.
625/49. SMITH, Jacob. £10 is to be given to the merchant who shall transport Jacob SMITH and his son to Virginia, when they are shipped. If the son be not shipped, then only £6 is to be paid and the remainder spent on apprenticing the son.

In the Principal Probate Registry, London.

P.C.C. 41 RUSSELL.

626, March 1.
PERSEY, Abraham, of Perseys hundred, Virginia, Esq., his will names Frances my wife, my brother John, Elizabeth and Mary my daughters.
POOLY, Mr Grevill, minister, and
KINGSMILL, Mr James, of James City Iland, gent.
RUSSELL, Mr Delyonell, my friend, of London, merchant.
SMYTHSON, Judith, my sister in England.
WEST, Nathaniel, my wife's son, under 21.
Administration 10 May, 1633, to
HILL, Mary, *alias* PERSEY, the daughter, Frances the relict having died.

In the Principal Probate Registry, London.

P.C.C. 78 SKYNNER.

1627, April 3.

MIDDLETON, Robert, who died in Virginia a bachelor, his will names William M., " my brother of Hamton in Yorkshire."
LANE, Edward, pulley maker, dwelling in Shadwell.
NORMANS, Alexander, of S^t. Katherine's, cooper, a debtor.
ANDREWES, Master Peter, his plantation.
BABB, Thomas, and
LOWTHER, Richard, overseers.
BLACKLER William, witness.
Admon., 18 July, 1627, to Thomas BABS.

In the Principal Probate Registry, London.

P.C.C. 45 BARRINGTON.

1627, April 11.

BURGES, John, the elder, of Westley " lyinge sicke in my bed in Richman's Iland in New England," his will gives " to Robert, John and William my sonnes my barke called The Annes with all her tackling, boate and provision and what she hath gained this summer. . . . My wife Joan whole executrix."
WITHERIDGE, John,
FORDE, James, and
NOTT, Edward, witnesses.
Proved at London 24 May, 1628, by Joan BURGES *alias* BRAY, the relict.

In the Principal Probate Registry, London.

P.C.C. 9 RIDLEY.

27, Oct. 12.
YARDLEY, Sir George, in his will names "my wife Temperance. This house in James Citty wherein I now dwell. This country of Virginia. My one thousand acres of land at Stanley in Warwicke River." Argoll my eldest son, Francis my sonne and Elizabeth YEARDLEY, all under 21.
PEIRSEY, Abraham.
HALL, Susanna, and
CLAYBORNE, William, scrivener, witnesses.
 Codicil, 29 Oct. 1627 : " My lands and houses within the Iland of James Citty."
 Admon. 14 Feb. 1628, to Ralph YARDLEY, the brother, during the minority of the children ; the relict " ab hac luce migravit," apparently in Virginia.

In the Principal Probate Registry, London.

P.C.C. 95 RUSSELL.

'27, Dec. 31.
MORDANT, George, of Fellingham, Norfolk, gent., in his will names my nephew Henry M., Esq., my dau. Marie, Lestrange my eldest son, and Robert, John, Henry and George. "All my adventure in Virginia."
PEPYS, Talbott, Esq., my brother.
WARD, Ralph, of Suffield, gent.
CASTLE . . . my brother, &c. &c. &c.
Proved at London 2 April, 1633.

In the Principal Probate Registry, London.

P.C.C. 40 SKYNNER.

A.D.

1627. SPELMAN, Thomas, gent., of Virginia, his will nuncupative was that his daughter Marye in Virginia should have all that he had here in England, and what he hadd in Virginia his wife should have.
BRIDGES, Jane.
ROWE, Mary.
SPELMAN, Fran., witnesses.
Admon 24 April, 1627, to Francis SPELMAN, the brother; the said deceased of Truro in Cornwall, in the absence of Hanna SPELMAN the relict in Virginia.

In the Principal Probate Registry, London.

P.C.C. 32 RIDLEY.

1628, June 26.
At Perye's Point, near James City, Virginia, the will of
PERREY, John, of St. Antholin, London, merchant, names St. Edmond Westgate, Exeter, Plymouth.
BRENTON, Seth, a fatherless child in Redderiff.
HARRISON, Susannah, d. of my cousin John.
HALSE, Mary, widow, my cousin.
BOURDON, Elizth, my cousin and her children.
WHITE, Ruth, my cousin.
CARTER, Susan, my cousin.
SYMONS, Alice.
PERY, Richard, my brother; W^m., a witness.
TUCKER, Thos. } my friends.
MARTIN, James }
BURBAGE, Thos., a witness.
Proved 28 Apl. 1629.

In the P.R.O., London.

CHANCERY BILLS AND ANSWERS.

CHARLES I. P. 68/60.

PERRY *v.* LOWE.

1628, July 2.

PERRYE, Richard, of London, merchant, and
HARRISON, Brian, of Wapping, mariner, and Susan his wife, late wife of
CARTER, James, master of the ship " Anne " of London. Voyage to Virginia.
LOWE, Ric., in Virginia, employed to collect CARTER's debts.

In the Principal Probate Registry, London.

P.C.C. 105 SCROOPE.

1629, Feb. 13.

WARNETT, Thomas, now of James Cittie in Virginia, merchant, in his will gives to
POTT, Mistris Elizabeth, one coife and crosse cloth of wrought gold ; to Dr. John POTT five thousand of severall sortes of nayles ; to Frances POTT fourscore pound of tobacco.
BOULTON, Mr Frauncis, minister.
JOHNSON, John, his wife.
BROWNING, John, his wife.
UPTONE, Mr John, his wife, one sea green scarfe edged with gold lace.
BURGESS, Mr Thomas, my second best sword, etc.
GREVETT, John, his wife.
KEYS, Thomas, his wife, one gilded looking glasse.
WANE, Sergeant John, his wife.
THOMPSON, Roger, his wife.
SYMES, Benjamin.

1629, Feb. 13—cont.
MULESTON, George.
GOUNDREY, John.
HATTONE, John.
SOUTHERNE, John.
BATT, Michael, his wife.
WARNETT, THomasina, my wife executrix.
STOME, James, overseer.
Proved at London 8 Nov. 1630, by the executrix.

In the Principal Probate Registry, London.

P.C.C. 52 SCROOPE.

1629, Sept. 3.
WRAXHALL, William, joiner, " being minded to go on a voyage to Virginia," names in his will " my wife Anne ; Mabell my daughter."
WARNER, John, scrivener,
ARMESTRONG, Richard, and
WILKINSON, Henry, are witnesses.
Proved at London 17 June, 1630, by Anne, the relict.

In the Principal Probate Registry, London.

P.C.C. 79 SCROOPE.

1629, Dec. 2.
RAYMENT, John, " in the shipp called The Friendshipp of London on a voyage to Virginia " made his will nuncupative naming " my kinsman dwelling at Wapping. My mother dwelling at Poole. My two sisters dwelling at Poole."
KENNEDE, Patrick, witness.
Admon. 2 Sept. 1630, to
GRAVES, Mary, *alias* RAYMENT, the relict.

Records of the Drapers' Company, London.

A.D.
1629. £6 13s. 4d. paid to Richard LANGELY, once Bridge Master, son of a member of the Court; he had been in Virginia.

Richard LANGLEY was son of John. (1626, P.C.C. 60 HELE.) Free 1613; married 1617 Alice LEICESTER. Aged 32 in 1620. (C. 24. 475/90.)
1626 "beyond the seas."
1641. Steward of Bethlehem Hospital.

In the Principal Probate Registry, London.

P.C.C. 81 SCROOPE.

1630, Aug. 20. At Great Hornemead in Hartfordshire.

WATERS, Edward, of Elizabeth City in Virginia, gentleman, his will names William my son to whom all my lands in Virginia, goods in England and Ireland. My brother John WATERS of Midleham in Yorkshire. Mrs Grace WATERS my now wife. Margaret WATERS my daughter.

ROWLSTON, Mr Lionel, of Elizabeth Cittie, gentleman.

PENNINGTON, M^r, my good friend att the Redd Lyon in Cheapside, London.

CAGE, Daniel and Phil., and

COLE, Solomon, witness.

Admon. 18 Sept. 1630, to John WATERS the brother, during the minority of William WATERS, the son.

In the Principal Probate Registry, London.

P.C.C. 164 LEE.

1630, Nov. 23.

ALTHAM, Emmanuel, "bound to the East Indies," in his will mentions "my brother Sir Edward ALTHAM," and

THOMSIN, M^{iss}, "in New England," to whom 40/s. is to be paid "which I doe of conscience owe to her although she knoweth it not."

In the Principal Probate Registry, London.

P.C.C. 66 PILE.

1631, Sept. 4.
BREWER, John, citizen and grocer of London, in his will names "my father Thomas BREWER." "To my son John BREWER my plantacon in Virginia called Stawley hundred *alias* Bruer's Burrough." Mary my wife, son Roger, daughter Margaret, brother Thomas and his children.

DRAKE, Mr Roger, my uncle, citizen and clothworker of London.

Admon. 13 May, 1636, to
BREWER, *alias* BUTLER, Mary, the relict, during minority of the children ; the testator having died in Virginia.

In the Principal Probate Registry, London.

P.C.C. 30 AND 34 GOARE.

1632, Dec. 7.
BURTON, George, of Stepney, Middlesex, "being bound on a journey to New England," a bachelor, his will names nephew Thomas, son of John BURTON.

ELLIS, Mr John, of S^t. Clement Danes, his house.

WARD, Stephen.

BURTON, John and Thomas, witnesses.

Admon. 27 Feb., 1636, to John, the brother, and John ELLIS, uncle on the mother's side of Thomas BURTON the nephew, by Sentence of the Court.

CROOKES, Sarah, *alias* BURTON, and
COOMBE, Amy, *alias* BURTON, the sisters, contested the will.

In the Principal Probate Registry, London.

P.C.C. 34 SADLER.

1633, Jan. 29.
CREED, John, of Martyn's hundred in Virginia, his will names my brother Cutbeard CREED.
PERRYOR, Joane, my sister.
CLARKE, Francis, my master.
FAUSSETT, Thomas, my master, executor.
WARD, Thomas, and
EDWARDS, Christopher, are witnesses.
   Admon. 18 April, 1638, to Ann, wife of Thomas FASSETT, now residing in Virginia.

In the Principal Probate Registry, London.

P.C.C. 75 SEAGER.

1633, Nov. 13.
PARKE, William, who died abroad, his will names Daniel, my youngest son, William my eldest son, Sarah my wife.
COLUMBELL, Francis, of London, merchant taylor.
FEILDEN, Nathaniel, of London, imbroderer.
STONE, James, of London, merchant.
BOUCHER, Daniel, purser of the good ship "The Blessinge."
THOROUGOOD, Adam, of Virginia, gent.
REY, Thomas, and
FELGATE, John, witnesses.
   Admon. 18 Aug. 1634, to Sara, the relict, during the minority of William, the son.

Records of Sandwich, Kent.

YEAR BOOKS C AND D, 1608–42.

1634, March 4 [*or a little later*].
In the ship " Hercules " of Sandwich, John WITHERLEY, master.
TILDEN, Nathaniel, of Tenterden in Kent, yeoman, Lidia his wief.
Children : Joseph, Thomas, Stephen, Marie, Sara, Judeth, Lidia.
Servants :
LAPHAM, Thomas.
SUTTON, George.
FORD, Edward.
JEAKINS, Edward.
COUCHMAN, Sara.
PERIEN, Marie.
BENNET, James.
AUSTEN, Jonas, of Tenterden, and Constance his wife.
Children : Jonas, Lidia ROBINSON-AUSTEN (*sic*), a little childe.
BROOKE, Robert, of Maidstone in Kent, mercer, and Anne his wief.
Children : Thomas, Samuel, Elys, Dorothie.
GALLANT, Abra & James.
HAYWARD, Thos., of Aylesford in Kent, taylor, & Susanna his wief.
Children : Thomas, John, Elizabeth, Susan, Martha.
WITHERELL, William, of Maidstone, schoolmaster, & Mary his wief.
Children : Samuel, Daniel, Thomas.
RICHARDS, Anne, servant.
WISE, Fannet not [Faintnot], Ashford, hempdresser.
BONEY, Thos., and
EWELL, Edward, shoemakers, of Sandwich.
HATCH, William, of Sandwich, merchant, & Jane his wief.
Children : Walter, John, Willm., Anne, Jane.
Servants :
HOLMES, W^m.
KETCHRELL, Joseph.
KETCRELL, Simon.
JENINGS, Robt.

1634, March 4—*cont.*
Servants (*cont.*):
SUTTON, Symon.
WELLS, Lidia.
HINCKLEY, Sam¹., of Tenterden & Sara his wief.
Children : Susan, Sara, Mary, & Elizab a kinswoman.
COLE, Isaac, of Sandwich, carpenter & Joane his wief.
Children : Isaac and Jane.
CHAMPION, Thos. of Ashford.
BESBEECH, Thos. of Ashford. Children : Mary & Alice.
EGELDEN, Elizab., Jane, Sara & John [in children column].
NEULEY, Thos. \
PACHEURY, Joseph } servants.
LOVE, Agnes /
LEWIS, John, of Tenterden & Sarah his wief, & child Sara.
HARRIS, Parnell, of the parish of Bow in London.
SAYERS, Jas. of Northbourne, Kent, taylor.
STARRE, Comfort, of Ashford in Kent, chirurgeon.
Children : Thomas, Comfort & Mary.
DUNKIN, Sam¹. \
TURKEY, John } servants.
STARRE, Truth shall prevail /
ROOTES, Joseph, of Great Chart.
MASON, Emma, of the parsh. of Eastwell, widow.
JOHNES, Margaret, wief of Willm., late of Sandwich, now of New England, painter.
BEST, John, of the same parish [S^t. George, Canterbury], taylor.
BRIGDEN, Thos., of the same town [Faversham], husbandman, and his wief and three children.

In the Public Record Office, London.

EXCHEQUER DEPOSITIONS.

10 CHAS. I. TRIN. 6.

1634, June 10.
Depositions at Dover, Kent.
RESTON, John, & Susan his wief, *v.*
BRAMES, Jacob and
NETHERSOLE, William.
Vessel called "The Silver Falcon," and proceeds of a voyage to Virginia.

In the Principal Probate Registry, London.

P.C.C. 97 GOARE.

1634, June 28.
WATKIN, Giffard, of London, merchant, "intending shortly to go a voyage beyond sea" [died unmarried in Virginia] his will names his brother Arthur, executor ; his mother living.
UNDERWOOD, John, scrivener, and
WILKES, William, are witnesses.
Proved at London 26 June, 1637, by Arthur WATKIN, the brother.

In the Principal Probate Registry, London.

P.C.C. 1 SADLER.

1634, July 10. At St. Marie's in the Province of Maryland.
CALVERT, George, Esq., third son to George CALVERT, Lord BALTIMORE, in his will names Leonard and Henry, my brothers, Ellen my sister.
COTTINGTON, Lord, and
ASHTON, Sir William, Knight, trustees.
BALTIMORE, Cecil, Lord, my brother.
PEASELEY, William, Esq., my brother.
GERRARD, Mr Richard, goods in Virginia and Maryland.
BOLES, Jo.
WELLS, John.
VAUGHAN, Robert, and
FENWICKE, Cuthbert, are witnesses.
Proved at London 19 Jan. 1634/5, by William PEASELEY.

In the Principal Probate Registry, London.

P.C.C. 38 SADLER.

1634, Dec. 24.
FELLGATE, Tobias, of Westover, Virginia, in his will nuncupative names his eldest son William, his daughter Sarah, his wife Sarah.
BLACKMAN, Mr Jeremy, was present.
MINIFEE, Mrs Elizabeth, dwelling in Virginia, £10.
BERRY, Tobias of, a youth, £40.
GREENE, M^r, overseer.
SWYER, Peter.
JONES, James.
PAGE, Roberte, and
SMITH, Solomon, witnesses.
Proved at London 23 April, 1635, by Sarah, the relict.

In the Principal Probate Registry, London.

P.C.C. 82 PILE.

1635, Jan. 6.

WHAPLETT, Thomas [died in Virginia], his will names his portion in the Chamber of London, sister Rebecca, uncle Thomas WHAPLETT.

REDMAN, John, friend, paid me for a plantacōn 1300 pound weight of tobacco. The executor for my estate in Virginia.

PEATE, Abraham, witness, to have half the said plantacōn.

MORTON, Mathewe, and

ANDREWES, Thomas, witnesses.

Proved at London 27 July, 1636, by Rebecca WHAPLETT the sister. Admon. 3 Nov. 1636, to Ralph GREGGE husband of Rebecca GREGGE *alias* WHAPLETT, now also deceased.

In the Principal Probate Registry, London.

P.C.C. 26 PILE.

1635, July 3.

ALLIN, Silvester, of the Tower liberty, London, "now bound out beyond the seas on a voyage to Virginia," names "my wife Elizabeth full executor."

AMREY, Edward, and

LACY, Frauncis, are witnesses.

Codicil, in the ship "The Transport" of London, 26 Aug.

CLARKE, Francis, and

TURWAY, John, witnesses.

Proved at London 22 March, 1635/6, by Elizabeth, the relict.

In the Principal Probate Registry, London.

P.C.C. 127 SADLER.

1635, Nov. 26.
MASON, John, of London, Esq., in his will wishes to be buried in S^t. Peter's, Westminster, gives legacy to poor of Southampton, names wife Anne, King's Lynn, Norfolk, " where I was borne." My county of New Hampshire or manor of Mason Hall in New England.

MOORE, Dorothie, my sister, and her children.
BALDWYN, Beatrice.
GREENE, Mr Josua, and his wife, my brother in law.
LAMBERT, Mr Edward, my brother in law and his wife.
BURTON, Mr Henrie, my brother in law and his wife.
WOLLASTON, Mr John, my brother in law and his wife.
MASON, Mr Robert, of Greenwich, his wife and mother, my cousins.
GEERE, Mr Thomas, and his wife, my cousins.
MASON, Thos, gent.
GIPPES, Mr Thos, and his wife, my cousins.
TUFTON, John, Anne, Robert and Mary, my grandchildren.
MASON, Dr Robert, my cousin, Chancellor of the diocese of Winchester. My lands at Capeham of Wagen upon the South side of Sagadahocke in New England called Masonia.

Proved at London 22 Dec. 1635, by Anne, the relict.

In the Principal Probate Registry, London.

P.C.C. 79 CAMBELL.

1635, Dec. 10.

GEERE, Dennis, of Sagust in Newe England, in his will names wife Elizabeth, daughters Elizabeth and Sarah. Plantations settled within the Patent of the Massachusetts.

PANKHUSRT, Ann, my cozen.

TUESLY, Elizabeth, £12.

CARVER, Roger, of Bridhemson [Brighthelmstone, Brighton] and RUSSELL, John, of Lewis in Sussex to sell my land in Old England.

TOPPER, Thomas
BRAINES, Thomas
LAUNDER, Thomas [All apparently of New England].
NYE, Benjamin
GRENNILL, Thomas

WINTHROP, John, elder, and
HUMPHRY, John, Esq^{rs}
WILSON, John, and
PETER, Hugh, preachers.
FREEMAN, Edward, and
GREENE, John, witnesses.
WINTHROP, Tho., governor.
DUDLEY, Tho., dep. governor.
ENDECOTT, Jo., attest.

Admon. 28 June, 1642, to Edward MOONCKE, uncle of Elizabeth and Sara GEERE; Elizabeth GEERE, the executrix named, having died.

In the Public Record Office, London.

DELEGATES' EXAMINATIONS.

VOL. 2.

BALTIMORE *v.* LEONARDS.

A.D.
1635. HAWLEY, Gabriel, of London, gent., aged 34, has lived there 5 years ; before that in Virginia ten months, and before that in London 5 years and more. (Signs.)
BALTIMORE, Lord, his house at the Upper end of Holborn; his brother and partner.
LEONARDS, Leonard, loaded into " The Ark," sailing to Maryland in Sept. 1633, divers tonnes of beer to the use of Lord BALTIMORE. There were three or four joined as partners in the said ship and her pinnace called " The Dove."
HALLY, Mr. Jerome, a partner in " The Ark," had an eighth part.
HALLEY, Gabriel, did bespeak and provide beer and victual for the ship.
CALVERT, Captain Leonard, partner in the pinnace.
CORNEWALLYS, Mr. Thomas, ditto.
SANDES or SAUNDERS, Mr. John, ditto.
BOULTER, John, citizen & skinner of London, of St. Botolph Aldgate, aged 40 ; has lived there 3 years, and before that for 12 years in the East Indies. Was purser and steward of the ship for the said voyage under the Lord BALTIMORE.
(Signs.)

Records of the Drapers' Company, London.

A.D.
1635. JARVES, Thomas, receives £1 "towards supplying his wants on going to Virginia." Made free of the Compy 1618; a tailor in Bishopsgate.

In the Principal Probate Registry, London.

P.C.C. 9 HARVEY.

1636, June 1.

HONYWOOD, John, of London, "intending a voyage by sea," his will names "my father Arthur HONYWOOD of Maidstone" and "my house at Langley in Kent." Uncle Anthonie H. his guift. Anthonie H., my brother deceased, Henry my brother, Jane my sister.

CLAYDON, Katherine, my sister.
CULPEPPER, Sir John.
DENNE, John, youngest son of my brother in law Thos. D., of Canterbury, gent.; Susan and Dorothie D., my sisters.
WATTS, Mary, my sister.
LANGWORTH, John.
HOPE, Francis, and
FLETCHER, Thomas, are witnesses.

Proved 23 Jan. 1638/9, by Thomas DENN; testator having died unmarried in America.

In the Principal Probate Registry, London.

P.C.C. 157 HARVEY.

1636, June 15.

BEHEATHLAND, John, "being about to goe to my mother in Virginia," his will names "my grandfather Mr Richard B., deceased, Charles B., my kinsman."

PEN, Pollider, my guardian.
ESLAKE, Samuel, and
VOYLEY, Thomas, are witnesses.

Admon. 22 Oct. 1639, to Charles B., the cousin.

In the Principal Probate Registry, London.

P.C.C. 187 HARVEY.

1636, Aug. 6.

HOOKER, Peeter, of London, tallow chandler, his will " intending a voyage to Virginia in the good shipp the Globb of London." To poor of Chilcombe, Hants.

STROUD, My Aunt.

EGER, My unckle, his children.

HOOKER, Anne, my cosen, my unckle Richard's daughter, & her brother Richard ; Henry HOOKER my uncle Peeter's son, his brother Nicholas ; said Peter's dau. Sibell HOOKER ; my brother John HOOKER and his son John.

WOOD, Richard, his children Hannah, John & Samuell.

HOOKER, Edward, my brother executor.

POTTER, Richard, and

STRETTON, George, witnesses.

Proved 22 Nov. 1639.

In the Principal Probate Registry, London.

P.C.C. 75 GOARE.

1636, Aug. 24.

ABBES, Edward [died in Virginia], his will names Thomas, my nephew, my wife Sara and my child.

BROWNE, Sara, daughter of Nicholas.

GOULDER, William, my man.

TODD, Robert, overseer.

BATT, Henry and William are witnesses.

Proved at London 23 May, 1637, by Sara, the relict.

In the Principal Probate Registry, London.

P.C.C. 198 HARVEY.

1636, Aug. 30.

ZOUCH, Sir John, Knight, his will names "my son John, bookes, armors, quilted coates and gunns." Laid out £1200 on my plantacon and ironworks. My dau. Isabella goods in Virginia. Elizabeth and Mary my daughters. "Isabella hath ventured her life in so dangerous a voyage."
HUTCHINSON, Sir Thomas.
LEAKE, Sir Thomas, of Little Leake.
BISPAM, M^r
ODINGSELLS, Mr Emanuell.
COKE, The Lady Theophila, my kinswoman and noblest friend.
WARD, Mr Gilbert, executor.
BIRON, Sir John.   BAKER, George.
LEECH, Sir Edward.   WHITE, Thomas.
RAMSAYE, Mr David.   LEWIS, Thomas, witnesses.
MASON, James.
Admon. 5 Dec. 1639, to John ZOUCH, the son.

In the Principal Probate Registry, London.

P.C.C. 54 GOARE.

1636, Aug. 31.

RING, John, of the city of London, yeoman, "now being in the ship called The Great Hopewell of London, bound for Virginia," in his will names "my brother Mathias RINGE plummer lyvinge in the Strand, London."
FLUELLINGE, Thomas, "living at the Pottashe Quarter in Virginia."
ATKINS, Master Richard, merchant; Abigall his wife.
BURNETT, Margaret, wife of Robert.
SHEMAND, Raphaell, the chirurgeon of the said shipp.
MORTH, Edward.
HAYNE, Richard, and
BAULKE, William, notary public, are witnesses.
Proved at London 10 April, 1637, by Matthew RINGE, the brother.

In the Principal Probate Registry, London.

P.C.C. 61 LEE.

636, Sept. 22.

GOODFELLOWE, Allen, of London, yeoman, " now bound to sea on a voyage to Virginia," his will names his mother Ann, brothers Christopher, William, John and Edward, sisters Mary and Elizabeth.
RAINSCROFT, Anne, my sister, wife of Mr R., upholder.
NEWMAN, Joane, wife of John.
KING, Henry, scrivener.
BURTON, Thomas, and
WALKER, John, are witnesses.
Proved at London 21 May, 1638, by Christopher GOODFELLOWE, the brother.

In the Principal Probate Registry, London.

P.C.C. 139 COVENTRY.

636, Nov. 11.

DEWELL, Edward, " of Warrasquoyke in Virginia, servant to
CORNOCKE, Symon, of the same," his will names " a mansion house being an Hoast howse or Inne " in St Mary's parish, Minstrell street, Redding, Berkes, England, late in the tenure of
MARCOMBE, Richard, my uncle, descending from my father George
DEWELL, being the signe of the " Rose."
ARMY, John,
SPACKMAN, Nicholas, and
CLAPPUM, William, are witnesses.
Proved by sentence at London 23 Nov. 1640, by
CURNOCKE, Simon, the executor named.
An Admon. granted June, 1637, to Humphrey DEWELL, the brother, being revoked.

In the Principal Probate Registry, London.

P.C.C. 52 GOARE.

1636, Nov. 21.

HOPKINSON, Daniell, in his will desires to be buried in Kicquatan church in Virginia, names his wife Sarah, brother Abraham, mother Katherine.

CLIFTON, Joseph, my brother, executor, to pay all seamen on board the "Tristram and Jane." My father and mother CLIFTON, sister Barbary CLIFTON.

MARKLAND, Michaell, my brother.

SOLE . . . my brother and sister.

HART, M^r

REEVES, Mr Robert, and

NANT, Thomas, are witnesses.

Proved at London 8 April, 1637, by Joseph CLIFTON.

In the Principal Probate Registry, London.

P.C.C. 140 TWISSE.

1636, Dec. 20.

BEARD, William, in his will names "my estate here in Virginia"; "my poor dear sister in Rye, Dorothy BEARD." Towards a new church in James City five hundredweight of tobacco. "My wicked wife Margaret."

CHILL, Mr Alexander, merchant at Billingsgate in London, executor.

CROWE, Thomas, estate of.

DOCKE . . . my sister in Rye.

KEMPE, M^r, the King's secretarie, "my nest of boxes."

MONES, Lawrence, Joves and Elizabeth.

BARKER, Mr William.

SWAN, Mr William, and

SHERLY, Mr Edward, to be overseers.

BARYHARD, Thomas, and

LOCKE, Thomas, are witnesses.

Proved at London 27 Oct. 1646, by Alexander CHILL.

In the Principal Probate Registry, London.

P.C.C. 21 PILE.

A.D.
636. SAMMES, Edward, of St. Helen's, London, names in his will, "my cousin STONE, preacher in New England."

In the Principal Probate Registry, London.

P.C.C. 87 LEE.

637, March 24.
PARRY, John, "whilst he lived inhabiting in Virginia," his will nuncupative names his brother William PARRY.
MINIFREY, M^r., his servant Samuel.
MARTIN, John.
PENDLE, Stephen.
HUNTER, Ralph, groom (witness).
JAMES, Josua (witness).
Proved 30 July, 1638.

Records of Sandwich, Kent.

YEAR BOOKS C AND D, 1608–42.

1637, May 11.

Persons which have taken passage from Sandwich for the American plantacons.

STARR, Thomas, of Canterbury, yeoman, Susan his wief & child Constant.
JOHNSON, Edward, of Canterbury, joyner, Susan his wief, children Edward, George, William, Matthew, John, Susan and Martha. Servants :
FARLE, John.
INGLAND, John.
NORCOTT, Ann.
BUTLER, Nicholas, of Eastwell, yeoman, Joyce his wief, children John, Henry, Lidia, and servants :
POPE, John.
GILL, John.
JENKIN, Richard.
ANGELLS, Marg[t].
SPICE, Christian.
HALL, Samuel, of Canterbury, yeoman, Joane his wife, & servants :
PAGE, Edw[d].
GRANGER, John & Grace.
BACHELOR, Henry, of Dovor, brewer, Martha his wief, & servants :
BUCKE, John & Susan.
TAYLOR, Sam[l].
WALKER, Margarie.
BACHELOR, Joseph, of Canterbury, taylor, Elizabeth his wife, child Marke BACHELOR and servants :
GRANGER, Tho[s].
HARNET, Edw[d].
CALL, Mary.
RICHARDSON, Henry, of Canterbury, carpenter, Mary his wief, children John, Henry, Elizabeth, Mary & Rachell.
BOYKETT, Jarvese, of Thanington, carpenter, & his servant :
GRANGER, Steven.

1637, May 11—*cont.*
BACHELOR, John, of Canterbury, taylor.
OVELL, Nathaniel, of Dovor, cordwinder, and his servant :
GRANGER, Thos.
CALLE, Thos., of Faversham, husbandman, Bennet his wief, & children Thomas, John & Margaret.
EATON, William, of Staple, husbandman, Martha his wief, and children John, Martha, Albe, & servant Jonas EATON.
COLEMAN, Joseph, of Sandwich, shoemaker, Sara his wief, and children Joseph, Zacharie, Sara, Mary.
SMITH, Mathew, of Sandwich, cordwinder, Sara his wief & children Mathew, John, Hanna, Elisabeth.
PEERCE, Marmaduke, of Sandwich, taylor, Mary his wief, and
HOOKE, John, his apprentice.
In witness, &c., 9 June, 1637.

In the Principal Probate Registry, London.

P.C.C. 47 LEE.

1637, July 7.
GONDRY, William, of London, gent., " now bound forth to Virginia in the good ship called ' The Rebecca,' of London," his will names
JEPSON, Susan, my sister, wife of Robert.
PRESTON, Anne, my mother, and
PALMER, Thomas, citizen and merchant taylor, executors.
JENNISON, William.
DEWER, John, servant to
WHEATLY, John, scrivener, and
LEWIN, Edward, are witnesses.
Proved at London 24 April, 1638, by Thomas PALMER, and 2 July, 1638, by Anne PRESTON, the mother.

In the Public Record Office, London.

CHANCERY AFFIDAVITS.

11/208.

1638, July 25.
KNOTT, James, of Mausanum in the lower Countie of Newe Norfolk in Virginia, gent, aged 35, resident there 20 yeares makes oath that
DALE, Sir Thomas, when Governor, caused the natives to pay yearly tribute of a bushel of corn. Elizabeth, Lady DALE his sole executrix. Deposes as to the massacre in Virginia.

In the Principal Probate Registry, London.

P.C.C. 169 LEE.

1638, Aug. 16.
STEELE, John, merchant, "arrived from Virginia in the good ship Anne and Susa," declared his will at Middlebourg in Zeland. He named
GOS, Marie, for service donne in his sicknes.
DESMEKER, Hester, & Mr John.
TIELROOS, Mary.
YSLEBEE, John.
CHATFEELD, Amyie, his wife.
HASE, Mr Joseph, merchant in London, tobacco.
BOREEL, Mr Adam, and.
GAGE, James, citizens of Middlebourg.
PALINGE, A., notary public.
Proved at London 11 Dec. 1638, by Anne STEELE, the relict.

In the Principal Probate Registry, London.

P.C.C. 9 HARVEY.

1638, Sept. 29.
Richard JONES belonging to the ship "Mayflower" of London, his will, "bound for St. Thomas."
AUSTIN, Elizabeth. His brothers Roger, John & Lewis, sisters Louise & Mary ; sister Elenor's children.
JONES, Rich^d. & Thomas.
WORCESTER, John.
CHESTER, John.
BRATHERIDGE, Thomas, my master.
JONES, Lewis, my brother, executor.
ANDREWES, Capt. Peter, my friend.
Proved 23 Jan. 1638/9.

In the Principal Probate Registry, London.

P.C.C. 102 HARVEY.

1638, Dec. 18.
MORECROFT, Edmund, of Virginia, merchant, his will names his sisters Elizabeth and Marie.
THURMER, Anne, my sister, John the younger, Elizabeth and Joane the younger, brother in law John THURMER.
HATT, Robert, and
LLOIDE, Cornelius, to administer here in Virginia.
THOMSON, Mr William, a debtor.
HOULDE, Robert, £10.
BLACKMAN, Mr Jeremia, and
CHURCH, William, to sell goods.
STALLINGE, Nicholas,
HANDSON, Richard, and
WEBB, John, are witnesses.
Proved at London 20 June, 1639, by Elizabeth MORECROFTE, the sister.

In the Public Record Office, London
High Court of Admiralty.

EXAMINATIONS 1/50.

A.D.
1638. CLEYBOURNE, William, of Virginia, Esq., deposes.

In the Public Record Office, London.

CHANCERY, TOWN DEPOSITIONS.

C. 24/640, NOS. 28 AND 47.

CARTER *v.* HOSKINS.

1639, Aug.-Oct.
LEE, Thomas, sailed for Virginia in 1634 on board "The James" with
PENNINGTON, William, who died in Virginia.
YARWORTH, John, cit. & clothworker of London, St. Alban's, Wood st., aged 55, & Elizabeth his wife, aged 53.
HOSKINS, Barth^w., gent. & wife of Elizabeth city.
WOODCOCK, John, cit. & scrivener of St. Mary Colechurch, part owner, aged 36.
LEE, Joane, wife of said Thomas, who died in Virginia.
GOTT, Richard, of Stepney, mariner, aged 32, deposes.
CARTER, John, married Joane, Thomas LEE's widow.
LEIGH, Richard (brother of said Thos. LEE) of St. Michael, Wood street, clothworker, aged 65, deposes.
ARCHER, Thos. cit. & leatherseller, aged 24, servant to
WILCOCKS, Thos., of Christchurch, London.

In the Public Record Office, London.

CHANCERY BILLS AND ANSWERS, CHARLES I.

B. 93/34. BARBER *v.* TAPP.

1639, Oct. 17.

BARBER *alias* GRIGG, Richard, of Beninton, Herts., yeoman, *versus* TAPP, Edmund, and others. TAPP declares that he left England 31 May, 1637, with all his family, arriving in New England the last day of July, having duly given warning of his departure to his landlord at Beninton.

CÆSAR, Sir Charles.
TAPP, Robert, his brother, and
LENCH, William, his kinsman, were his trustees.

Sworn at Quinypyack in New England 7 Aug. 1640 before the Commissioners.

EATON, Theoph.
GREGSON, Thomas.
LEACH, Edmund. [Answer of Robert TAPP is filed B. 86/3.]

In the Public Record Office, London.

CHANCERY AFFIDAVITS.

12/329.

1640, May 14.

NORTON, Francis, of New England in America makes oath that MASON, Anne, of East Greenwich, Kent, widow, in Feb. 1638 demised to

HOUGHTON, Robert, cit. & brewer of London, her part of land in or near the River of Piscataway *als.* Pascatta Quakke in New England for 5 years. Rent £25 p.a.

[*Note.*—Francis NORTON was a haberdasher of London.]

In the Principal Probate Registry, London.

P.C.C. 81 EVELYN.

1640, Nov. 9.

CRADOCK, Mathew, of London, merchant, in his will names S^t. Peter le Poor "where I served my apprenticeship," S^t. Swithins, "where I now dwell"; wife Rebecca, daughter Damaris; house at Rumford, Essex; estate in New England, America; brother Samuell, his wife and sons Samuell, now at Emanuel College, Cambridge, and Mathew.

BEMISTER, Stephen, late of London, clothworker, deceased.
BUTLER, John,
WEBB, Thomas and Edward, and
DAVIS, Thomas, clothier, creditors.
COLTHURST, Henry, son of Thomas, deceased, a creditor.
PENNOYER, Mr William, to settle accounts.
SAWYER . . . my brother and sister, and her daughter Dorothy.
JORDAN, Hannah, my cosine, now dwelling with me.
HODILINE, Thomas, and
LEWES, Edward.
COKAYNE, Mr William, to assist my wife.
BUDS, Edward,
ALVEY, William, and
HOVELL, Richard, are witnesses.

Proved at London 4 June, 1641, by Rebecca CRADOCKE, the relict.

In the Principal Probate Registry, London.

P.C.C. 115 EVELYN.

1641, Sept. 6.

BARHAM, Anthony, " of Mulbery Iland in Virginia, gent. ; and at this present resiant in England," his will names his wife Elizabeth and daughter Elizabeth.

LYNE, Mr Thomas, debtor for £226 10s.

BENNETT . . . my mother and brother in law Richard B.

DUKE, Mrs Mary, my sister.

GRAVES . . . , my sister, her son.

MAIOR, Edward, my friend and Martha his wife ⎫ executors in
BUTLER, William, my loving friend and gossipp, ⎬ Virginia.
and his daughter Sara. ⎭

PERCE, Mrs Joane, wife of Mr William.

ALDEY, Mr Edward, minister of St Andrew's in Canterbury.

DOVES, Thomasine,

COLLYNS, Thomas,

MYNS, Katherine, and

BARLOWE, Richard, scrivener, are witnesses.

Proved at London 16 Sept. 1641, by MAIOR and BUTLER.

In the Public Record Office, London.

EXCHEQUER DEPOSITIONS.

17 CHAS. I. MICH. 29.

1641, Sept. 27.

LAVINGTON, Miles, of the Custom House, Bristol, *v.*

ROGERS, Brian, merchant,

PENNOYER, William, merchant.

Importation of tobacco from Virginia forbidden, except to the Port of London.

In the Principal Probate Registry, London.

P.C.C. 80 CAMBELL.

1642, May 28.

BRIDGES, Francis, of Clapham, Surrey, citizen and salter, of London; his will names his wife Sara, estate in Lachingdon, Essex, and S^t. Sythes, London.
BENSON, Elizabeth, my sister and her four children [namely]
RISBY, William and Judith,
PENNINGTON, Elizabeth, and (Daniel P., in Bow churchyard, London)
THORNE, Sara.
HUNTLEY, Oliver, my cousin german; Humfrey H., son of William.
BARTON, John, my cousin.
CLAYTON, Constance, my cousin.
WHEELER, Susan, my cousin.
CARPENTER, Susan, my wives mother; Gabriell my brother in law.
BICKE, Marie, my sister in law; Wm. BEEKE my brother in law.
OFFSPRING, Mr Charles, minister, my cousin.
CANNON, Isaac, my now servant.
WALKER, Thomas, sometyme my servant; Thos W., my brother in law.
BOND, Margaret, sometyme my servant.
BOWLES, Elizabeth, sometyme my servant.
TAYLOR, Mr Francis, parson of Clapham.
ARTHUR, Mr John, our new Lecturer.
PEMBERTON, M^r, minister.
WELLS, M^r, curate of Battersey.
WASHBORNE, Mrs Mary, widow, the elder.
BONNER, Samuel, my wives kinsman; Henry B., my brother in law.
HARRIS, Elizabeth, my wives cousin.
REMNANT, Samuel and Sarah, children of William, under 21.
WELLS, M^r
HOOKER, M^r

1642, May 28.—*cont.*

PETERS, M^r, and
SYMS, M^r, ministers of New England, £50 for the enlargement of a College in New England and £20 for clothing the poor there.
SHAWE, Anthony.
SOLE, John,
HATHAWAY, George,
RABASHA, John, and
CARPENTER, Ga., are witnesses.
Proved at London 23 June, 1642, by Sara, the relict.

In the Principal Probate Registry, London.

P.C.C. 111 CAMBELL.

1642, June 2.
COOKE, Samuel, of Dublin, Ireland, his will names Anne my wife, messuage called Rowses, lands in S^t. Andrew's and Ringsfield, Suffolk, son John, dau. Anne, brother John. Recites indentures 19 April 7 Charles, Erasmus COOKE [my brother] and
FISKE, William, of Norton, gent.; John of Ruttesden, Suffolk, gent., my kinsman.
CHAPLAINE, Clement, of Wetherfield in New England, my kinsman, and
NORRIS, Tobias, of Dublin, gent., executors.
DUDLEY, Augustine, and
KETT, Philip, are witnesses.
Proved at London 29 Sept. 1642, by Erasmus and Thomas COOKE.

In Canterbury Probate Registry.

CONSIST. CANTERBURY FILE 1644 NO. 55.

The Will of Trustram STEVENS *of Dover, mariner.*

A.D.

1643. STEVENS, Trustram, of Dover, mariner, "ready to go to sea"; born at Brixton, Devon; his house & key near the sign of the Falcon.
STEVENS, Robert, eldest son, to whom lands in Petham.
STEVENS, Trustram, second son, to whom lands without Cowgate.
STEVENS, Richard, third son.
CHALKE, William, and Sarah his wife.
PENNY, Edward, of the Flower-de-Luce in Dover.
STOPGATE, . . . a Dutchman.
STREETING, Mildred.
HOOKER, John, shipwright.
STEVENS, Denance, testator's mother.
STEVENS, Robert, decd., testator's father, had Stowe in Brixton.
STEVENS, Trustram, " youngest " son of testator.
LUCAS, William, his house " on the peere at Dover."
STEVENS, Frances, testator's wife, dau. of
MARTEN, John, deceased, & Katherine his wife.
STEVENS, William, & John, testator's brothers.
STERT, John, " cosen."
(Trustram STEVENS was brother-in-law of Tristram COFFIN, who went to New England.)

In the Public Record Office, London.

CHANCERY PROCEEDINGS.

644, July 4.   c. 24. 683/41.

TRERISE, Nicholas, of Charlestown, Virginia, returned about July, 1640, from Virginia to London in the ship "Planter," laden with hogsheads of tobacco to the value of £200. (JAUNEYE *v.* TRERISE.)

In the Public Record Office, London.

DELEGATES' EXAMINATIONS.

VOL. 2.

JACKSON *v.* BATEMAN.

Seizure of the "Mary" at Charlestown.

A.D.

644/5. ALDWORTH, John, of St. Leonard's, Bristol, merchant, aged 19; born there; hath lived 5 years with Mr. Hugh BROWNE, merchant, as an apprentice; Mr. Joseph JACKSON is Mr. BROWNE'S partner. (Signs.)

JACKSON, Philip, brother of Joseph, and correspondent in Spain, at Bilboa. ALDWORTH believes he has not been in England these five years.

BROWNE, Hugh, of St. Leonard's, Bristol, merchant, aged 40, has lived there 5 years and before that in St. Stephen's; born in Bristol. He and Joseph JACKSON, in April last set out in the ship the "Mary" from Bristol to New England to take in Fish, etc., and go to Bilboa. Producents desired to draw their estate from Bristol since the King's taking of it, to London, and are men well affected to the Parliament. Suffered much loss for such their good affection, to the sum of £800. (Signs.)

GWYN, John, of St. Mary Port, Bristol, mariner, aged 25, born there. Was master of the ship "Mary." BROWNE and JACKSON would have gone to New England could they have

A.D.
1644/5.—cont.

conveyed their estates and children thither, Mr. BROWNE and Mr. JACKSON were Sheriffs of Bristol at the taking of the city, and Hugh BROWNE was questioned for his life by the King's party and fined £1200.

RUSSELL, Mr., resided with his family in New England for divers years, and

ABLEY, Mr., employed in New England, as factors or agents for BROWNE and JACKSON. His wife and family remained in Bristol. The "Mary" was forcibly taken in the river of Charlestown contrary to the government there.

STAGG and Company took and surprised the "Mary," and were refractory to all persuasions, STAGG saying that he would not vary from his Commission, by which the trade of New England is much disturbed.

WOREY, Ralph, of Charlestown in New England, merchant, aged 29, has lived there 3 years, before that in Bristol 20 years, born at Bedminster, near Bristol. The "Mary" did lie in Charlestown River near this deponent's door. If the business had come to a fight the town might have been in danger of being beaten down. STAGG seized the ship to the great terror and affrightment of the town. (Signs.)

WHETCOMBE, Benjamin, of London, merchant, aged 25, has lived there 20 years; born at Woodbury, Devon. (Signs.)

GIFFORD, George, of St. Olave, Hart Street, London, clothier, aged 38, has lived there 3 years, before that at Bilboa in Spain 10 years, born at Northian, Devon. (Signs GIFFARD.)

JOHNSON, Edward, of Stepney, Middx., sailor, aged 21, has lived there since his birth. Was one of Capt. STAGG's mates at the taking of the ship "Mary," and came home Master in the said prize ship. (Signs.)

CAPELL, George, of Stepney, mariner, aged 32, has lived there 3 years; before that at Littleham, Devon, where he was born. Was quartermaster of the "Elizabeth," of London, whereof Stagg was commander, when the "Mary" was seized. The Court was kept at Salem, twelve miles off from where the ship lay in July, 1644. (Signs.)

Parish Register of St. Dunstan's, Stepney, Middlesex.

1645, Oct. 23.
MOORE, Richard, of Salem in New England, maryner, and WOOLNO, Elizabeth, of Lymehouse, married.

In the Principal Probate Registry, London.

P.C.C. 30 GREY.

1645, Dec. 24.
NELSON, Thomas, of Rowlay, Essex, in New England, " now about to voyage into Old England," his will names " Joane my wife."
Mill in Rowlay and land lately in occupation of
WORMEHILL, Joseph.
ROGERS, M^r., " ground in the Pound field next."
NELSON, Philip, Thomas & Marie, my sons and daughter.
BULLINGTON, or BELLINGHAM, Richard,Esq.
DUMER, Richard, my uncle.
WITHAM, Kath., my aunt.
ROGERS, M^r. Ezeckiell, of Rowley, and
NORTON, M^r. John, of Ipswich, overseers.
HOWCHIN, Jeremy, and
NORTHENS, Ezeckiell, witnesses.
NELSON, Samuel, my son, named in Codicil, 1648.
SCATCHELL, Goodman, from whom testator bought a farm.

In the Principal Probate Registry, London.

P.C.C. 113 PEMBROKE.

1646, Sept. 15.
HARVEY, Sir John, Knight (a bachelor), his will names " sums due to me from several persons in Virginia." Symon, eldest son of my late brother Sir Symon H. of London. " My daughters Ursilla & Ann." Admon. 16 July, 1650, to Alice, widow of Tobias DIXON. Testator died " beyond the seas."

In the Principal Probate Registry, London.

P.C.C. 86 ESSEX.

1647, Oct. 20.

CLARKE, Agnes, of Ayshill, Somerset, widow; her will names
HARVEY, William, son of Thomas, deceased, "my kinsman," now
in New England. James his brother.
Proved 10 May, 1648.

In the Principal Probate Registry, London.

P.C.C. 10 GREY.

1650, Jan. 23.

PARKS (PERKS), Edward, citizen & merchant taylor of London, in
his will names, wife Maria, sons Henry, Edward, John, William,
Stephen, Thomas, Dannett, Francis & Samuel. I now dwell
in Stepney in the N.W. part of the great messuage formerly of
WORCESTER, Henry, Earl of.

WILCOX, Anne, my sister, and her children Mark, Francis, Susan
& Anne.

PLAMPIN, Marie, my dau., now wife of Thomas, & her children
Thomas & Edmond PLAMPIN.

FORTH, William & Daniel, my brothers, both of London, woollen-
drapers, overseers.

CRAWLEY, Marie, widow, the relict took administration 3 Nov.
1681.

Parish Register of St. Nicholas Acons, London.

1650-51, Jan. 28.

BUTLER, John, of New England, and
PARDIE, Mary, of Bransted in the Countie of Hamshere, married;
friend of
COOPER, John.

In the Principal Probate Registry, London.

P.C.C. 153 WOOTTON.

651, July 24.

PECKE, Robert, minister of the word of God at Hingham, Norfolk, in his will names "the children of
MASON, Anne, my daughter, wife of Captain John, of Seabrooke on the river Connecticot in New England."

In the Principal Probate Registry, London.

ARCHD. COLCHESTER, 1650-52, NO. 106.

A.D.
651. GAUDEY, Richard, of Colchester, Essex, saymaker, in his will names his son Thomas, of Halstead, weaver,
CHATERTON, Edward, & his two sisters in Holland, his grandchildren; his sister Susanna CHATERTON,
GAUDEY, Mary, his daughter "that went to Newe England," and his wife Elizabeth GAUDEY.

In the Principal Probate Registry, London.

P.C.C. 243 BOWYER.

652, April 2.

PERRY, Robert, of Bristol, clerk; his will names
MORGAN, Temperance, my kinswoman, wife of Rich^d. M. of Chepstow.
MORDEN, Elizth., my kinswoman, wife of Rich^d. M. of Chepstow.
PERRY, Robert, son of my sister Elizabeth, *living in Virginia.*
WEBB, William, son of my kinsman W^m. W.
JONES, Richard, my cosen & his wife.
BENTLY, William, my brother in law & his wife. Robt. B. my godson.
HILL, Philip, my cosen, & his wife.
MEDOWES, Marian, my kinswoman, wife of Marrian (*sic*) M. & others.
Proved 2 July, 1652, by relict Elizabeth.

Parish Register of West Drayton, Middlesex.

1653, Feb. 27.
BRUISTER, John, a Virginian, and
EVERID [or DUERID], Jane, married.

In the Principal Probate Registry, London.

P.C.C. 301 WOOTTON.

1655, Feb. 9.
SHURT, George, of Bideford, Devon, marchant, in his will names
SHURT, Abraham, " my brother now in New England God sending him home from thence to live in Bideford."

In the Principal Probate Registry, London.

P.C.C. 130 WOOTTON.

1655, March 18.
NOYES, Anne, of Cholderton, Wilts., widow, in her will names " my sons James and Nicholas now in New England and their children."

In the Principal Probate Registry, London.

P.C.C. 301 WOOTTON.

1655, May 1.
SEARLE, Jane, of Otterton, Devon, widow, in her will names
MASON, Jane, and
VEREN, Mary, " my daughters in New England."
CONANT, Richard, my son, executor.
[Jane SEARLE was widow of Richard CONANT (ob. 1625), and connected with New England.]

In the Principal Probate Registry, London.

P.C.C. ADMON. ACTS, 1655.

1655, May 21.

HARVEY, Robert, a bachelor, late in New England. Administration to
DORRELL, Margaret, wife of John (then beyond the seas), his cousin-german.

In the Principal Probate Registry, London.

P.C.C. 36 WOOTTON.

1656, Jan. 7.

ALLEN, James, of Kempston, Bedford, blacksmith, in his will names Roger ALLEN my son, " nowe livinge in Newe England."
DEWLITTLE, Abram, & my daughter Joane his now wife, " living now also in New England."

In the Principal Probate Registry, London.

P.C.C. 2 WOOTTON.

1656, Feb. 3.

WHEELER, Richard, citizen and innholder of London ; his will names
MOYE, Richard, & his brother John now in Virginia, testator's grandchildren. Property in Moorefields, London, called " The Cock in the Hole." Relatives in Wiltshire.

In the Principal Probate Registry, London.

P.C.C. 152 WOOTTON.

1656, Sept. 30.

NORCROSS, Jeremiah, in his will names " estate in New England left in the hands of my friend
CHADDOCKE, Charles, of New England."

In the Principal Probate Registry, London.

P.C.C. 115 WOOTTON.

1657, Feb. 11.
HITCH, Mildred, of S^t. John Evangelist, London, widow, her will names
JOHNSON, Mary, my kinswoman, of New England, formerly
HAZARD, Mary, her children John, Rebecca & Hannah H.

In the Principal Probate Registry, London.

P.C.C. 128 WOOTTON.

1657, Aug. 20.
TOPPING, Richard, of Soulbury, Bucks., in his will names " my son Richard and four of my children which I have in New England," daughter Lidia, two younger sons Joseph and Benjamin, under 21. Wife Alice.

In the Principal Probate Registry, London.

P.C.C. 198 WOOTTON.

1657, Sept. 3.
ENSIGNE, Thomas, of Cranbrook, Kent, yeoman; his will names "my father Thomas ENSIGNE in Nue England." "My brother and sisters in Nue England."

In the Principal Probate Registry, London.

P.C.C. 128 WOOTTON.

1657, Sept. 5.
COCHET, Robert, of Mickleover, Derby, gent., in his will names
JOYCE, Dorothy, my sister, wife of John, of New England, and their children.

In the Principal Probate Registry, London.

P.C.C. 3 WOOTTON.

1657, Nov. 20.
HAWKER, George, of St. Martin's, Ludgate, London, combmaker; his will names "my brother Edward HAWKER living in Virginia."

In the Principal Probate Registry, London.

P.C.C. 109 WOOTTON.

1657, Dec. 2.
CHAUNCY, Judith, of Yardley, Herts., spinster; her will names Mr. Charles, my brother, "minister of God's word and now living in New England." His sons Isaac & Ichabod. His sixe children "as I am informed."

In the Principal Probate Registry, London.

P.C.C. 115 RUTHEN.

A.D.
1657 BATE, Richard, of Lydd, Kent, jurate, in his will names "my mother Alice BATE in New England."

In the Principal Probate Registry, London.

P.C.C. 213 RUTHEN.

A.D.
1657. GORGES, John, Esq., of St. Margaret, Westminster; his will mentions lands in Somerset. My patent of the Province of Mayne, New England.

In the Principal Probate Registry, London.

P.C.C. 141 RUTHEN.

A.D.
1657. HOPKINS, Edward. His will mentions estate in New England and friend
EATON, Theophilus, Esq.

In the Principal Probate Registry, London.

P.C.C. 456 RUTHEN.

A.D.
1657. LUCAS, Bridget, wife of Edward, citizen & plaisterer of London; her will mentions John BISHOP her brother, and
BISHOP, Mary, her kinswoman, in Virginia.

In the Principal Probate Registry, London.

P.C.C. 282 WOOTTON.

1658, March 25.
GROOME, John, of Strood, Kent, gent., in his will names
OLIVER, Capt. Jas., of New England and "what estate in cattle I have in New England."

In the Principal Probate Registry, London.

P.C.C. 296 WOOTTON.

1658, April 29.
TRAHERNE, William, of S^t. Clement Danes, Middx. chaundler, in his will names
TRAHERNE, Richard, "my brother, now in Virginia."

In the Public Record Office, London.

STATE PAPERS MISC. DOM., AND FOREIGN, NO. 26.

A.D.
1662/3. "CHAFFEY a New England preacher lives and meetes in Wapping."

"HARWOOD, Jo, a merc^t. at Mileend Green, a factious dangerous Independent & ye com'on factor for all ye merch^{ts} tradeing, especially to N. Engl^d., who uses constantly to cover & disguise ye Shipps, Goods & persons of those of y^t opinion, in their voyages and passages, so as ye Offic^{rs} of ye Customes &c at Gravesend & oth^r places are by his interest & money corrupted to slipp ye Oathes, wch otherwise ought to be tendred to all persons going out, &c. Mr. SCOTT."
(Sir Joseph WILLIAMSON'S ' Spy Book.')

In the Principal Probate Registry, London.

P.C.C. 46 HYDE.

1663, Dec.
CHEESMAN, John, of S^t. Mary Magdalen, Bermondsey, Surrey, gent., his will.
To godchild Anna CHEESMAN "plantations in the county of Gloucester in the continent of Virginia."
Proved 2 May, 1665.

In the Public Record Office, London.

DELEGATES' EXAMINATIONS, VOL. 10.

CLERKE *v.* VASSALL.

A.D.
1668. BIGG, Eliz[th]., of London, spinster, aged 22, born in S[t]. Leonard's Shoreditch, deposes that
VASSALL, Henry, in Feb. 1666, on board the ship "Marygold," bound for Virginia, said to his father Samuel VASSALL, "Sir, I give unto you all that I have in the world." He was a merchant and very discreet; an able person and could write well. Has known Francis VASSALL for several years. Her mother was present in the said ship.
WILLIAMSON, Thomas, was present, of London, haberdasher, aged 28; born at Saffron Walden, Essex.
CLIFFE, Charles, an infant, maintained by Mr. WILLIAMSON. Mary CLIFF. WILLIAMSON deposes that the legacy to Elizabeth BIGG was ordered by the Governor of Virginia to be paid.

In the Public Record Office, London.

DELEGATES' EXAMINATIONS, VOL. 10.

CLERK *v.* VASSALL.

A.D.
1669. BRACE, Philip, of St. Giles in Fields, gent., aged 45, born in London, says that
WILLIAMSON, Thomas, deposed that he never was possessed of any of the estate of
VASSALL, Henry, deceased. Frances VASSALL exhibited a Bill in Chancery against WILLIAMSON. Samuel VASSALL died much in debt, was father of Francis and Henry.
CLIFF, Mary, when her husband was killed was left in a low and mean condition.
BIGG, Mrs. Elizabeth, said that Henry VASSALL'S goods were apprized in Virginia.
HARDIE, John, of London, citizen & surgeon, aged 24, born there, deposes that in 1666 he was chirurgeon on board "The Marygold" bound for Virginia.
PENSAX, Captain Henry, master.
HORNE, Mr. Robert, was aboard & witness to Henry VASSALL'S will.

In the Principal Probate Registry, London.

P.C.C. ADMONS. 1670.

1670, July 4.
PERRY, Thomas, of Virginia. Administration to
TERRETT, Margaret (wife of Bartholomew), the sister.

In the Public Record Office, London.

EXCHEQUER DEPOSITIONS.

24 CHAS. II, EASTER 17.

1672, Feb. 12.
SANCARFE, Walter, master of the ship "Margery" of Dover, which made the voyage to Virginia. Whether identical with the ship "S^t. John" taken by the "Oxford" frigate in 1667. Depositions taken at Amsterdam.

Parish Register of Lancaster, Lancashire.

1674, July 9.
CAREY, Nathanyall, and
WALKER, Elizabeth, of Charlstowne in New Ingland, married.

In the Principal Probate Registry, London.

P.C.C. 128 BATH.

1678, Dec. 15.
GRENDON, Thomas, of S^t. James, Duke's Place, London, citizen and draper; his will names
GRENDON, Thomas, my grandson, now in Virginia, lands in Fultherly in Shenston, co. Stafford.
DUKE, Hannah, my daughter in Virginia.

Parish Register of St. Dunstan, Stepney, Middlesex.

1687, Aug. 18.

ASHCOM, Charles, of Pensilvania in America, bachelor, and EARLE, Martha, of Ratcliffe, spinster, married.

In the Principal Probate Registry, London.

P.C.C. 1 ENT.

1688, June 30.

BAWDON, Sir John, of London, merchant, his will. Lettetia his now wife (dau. of Edwd. Popham, Esq.). Estate in New England, Barbados, Nevis.
Proved 8 Jan. 1688/9.

In the Principal Probate Registry, London.

P.C.C. 167 FANE.

1689, Dec. 10.

GRAVE, John [a Quaker], in his will refers to "debts due to me here in Virginia." "Our meeting house on Lenyneck Field." Nephew Peter GRAVE.

MURRAY, John, executor.
ALLEN, Arthur, debtor.
PROUD, Thomas.
MURRAY, Elizabeth ; John, W^m. & George, three sons of John M.
BRESSIE, Susan. LEWIS, W^m., wife, & son John.
NEWTON, Samuel. TABURY, Thos. ⎫
HARRIS, John. CARRELL, J^{no}. ⎪
GREWES, Peter. MILLER, Edwd. ⎬ witnesses.
RICHARDS, William. WILSON, W^m. ⎪
LUX, John. PROUD, Thos. ⎭
MILLER, Sarah.
POTTER, Walter, my sister's son.
Proved 24 Sept. 1692 by Walter POTTER.

In the Public Record Office, London.

CHANCERY BILLS AND ANSWERS BEFORE 1714.

HAM. 280/31.

PERRY *v.* GODART.

1692, May 24.
PERRY, Micajah, and
LANE, Thomas, of London, merchants, complain that
PARKE, Daniel, of Virginia, left his daughter Rebekah £1500 at 18 or marriage; his son Daniel under 21 and made
CARTER, Edward, his executor; in Nov. 1685 Rebekah married
GODART, John, of London, merchant, to whom the executors or trustees paid money, but he refuses to give plaintiffs a release.

In the Public Record Office, London.

CHANCERY BILLS AND ANSWERS BEFORE 1714.

MITFORD 355/15.

PERRY *v.* BLAND.

1693, Dec. 23.
PERRY, Micajah, and
LANE, Thomas, of London, merchants, complain that being correspondents in Virginia for
HARRISON, Benjamin, of Southwark, Surrey, merchant, in Oct. 1691
BLAND, Sarah, relict of John, of London, merchant, and
POVEY, Thomas, of Westminster, executor of John BLAND, treated respecting the Berkeley Plantation in Westover, Virginia, for
HARRISON, agreed to pay £180 down, and £180 by bond to
GREEN, John, Esq., brother to Sarah BLAND.
HARTWELL, Henry, of James City, merchant.
BLIGHTON, Thomas, and
MING, James, of Charles City, gent., attornies for the executors.

In the Public Record Office, London.

CHANCERY BILLS AND ANSWERS BEFORE 1714.

REYN 322/42.

PHILLIPS *v.* PERRY.

1697/8, March 10.
PERRY, Micajah, his answer to the Bill of Complaint of
PHILLIPS, William, and others ; says that
Cox, John, built a ship in Virginia called the " Nansimum "
   frigate. Voyage to London. Dispute with Richard Cox,
   father of John, and administrator of Richard and Thos.
   Cox his sons.
FIDLER and
JEROM requested PERRY to adjudicate, and pay FIDLER and the
   seamen.

Note.—Richard Cox of Great Coxwell, Berks, gent., was father of John, according to Reyn, 278/68, SCOTT *v.* PERRY.

In the Public Record Office, London.

CHANCERY BILLS AND ANSWERS BEFORE 1714.

REYN. 282/88.

JEROME *v.* PERRY.

1698, May 11.
PERRY, Micajah, his Answer to the Bill of Complaint of
JEROM, Stephen, Esq. Refers to agreement 1 Aug. 1694 between
Cox, Richard, of S^t. Thomas, Southwark, gent., and his brother
Cox, Thomas, of Virginia, merchant, the said JEROM and
SAPSFORD, John, of Deptford, shipwright, Benjamin JEROM and
LOCK, Edward, agree to sail for Virginia, there to build a ship for
   the said Richard and Thomas Cox.

In the Public Record Office, London.

DELEGATES' EXAMINATIONS.

VOL. 23, NOS. 15 AND 17.

A.D.
1698. HACKETT, or HASKETT, Stephen, brother of Elias, sen^r., was put apprentice to a soap-boiler, married Elizabeth HILL, and went to Salem in New England.
CRUMSEY, Mary, wife of Lewis, a great-niece of Elias (signs CRUMZE) deposes.
HACKETT, Elias, son of Stephen and nephew of Elias, sen^r., married Elizabeth RICH and settled in Barbados ; trades in shipping and merchandise. (Signs.) Mary, wife of Elias, sen^r., died a few days before him. Stephen and Elizabeth had a dau., Elizabeth, and daughters Mary, Sarah, Hannah and Martha, now at Salem.

In the Principal Probate Registry, London.

P.C.C. 145 FOX.

1699, Spt. —.
HARVEY, William, of Stepney, Middx., master of the merchant ship "The Baily," died in Virginia ; his will names wife Johanna, mother, brothers and sisters.
PENEY, —, my daughter.
PORE, —, my aunt.
Proved 27 July, 1716, by Johanna, the relict.

In the Public Record Office, London.

CHANCERY BILLS AND ANSWERS BEFORE 1714.

HAM. 611/34.

PARKE *v.* PERRY.

1701, June 20.
PARKE, Daniel, of S^t. Margaret's, Westminster, Esq., complains that in 1688 he resided in Virginia as a merchant.
PERRY, Sarah, now wife of Richard P., of London, tobacconist, and dau. of
RICHARDS, George, of London, tobacco-merchant, who died in 1695, sues on a bond which has long since been paid.

In the Public Record Office, London.

CHANCERY BILLS AND ANSWERS BEFORE 1714.

COLLINS 321. COX *v.* PERRY.

1701, June 27.
COX, John, mariner, complains that in 1695 he built a ship at Nancy Mumm, Virginia, called " The Nancy Mumm " frigate to take tobacco to London.
PERRY, Micajah, a wealthy man, has converted ship and cargo to his own use.

In the Principal Probate Registry, London.

P.C.C. 53 DEGG.

1702, Jan. 20.
LOWE, Micajah, of Charles City, Virginia, his will, now of Carchaulton, Surrey, merchant. Wife Sarah.
PERRY, Micajah, " my uncle."
HAMLIN, Mrs. Elizabeth, " my mother in law."
LOWE, Susannah and Mary, " my sisters."
JARRETT, Johannah, " my sisters."
MORGAN, Captaine Christopher and James, " my friends."
Proved 17 May, 1702/3.

In the Public Record Office, London.

CHANCERY PROCEEDINGS.

C. 24. 1253/12.

1703, March 14

SELLECK, Robert, of New York in America, merchant, aged 23, now lodging at " The George " inn, Drury Lane.

GLEN CROSS, William, of the same, merchant, aged 31, now lodging at Mr. Broughton WRIGHT'S in Ball Alley, Lombard street, depose.

In the Public Record Office, London.

CHANCERY PROCEEDINGS.

C. 24. 1266/15.

A.D.

1703. HAMLIN, Richard, of Ratcliffe, mariner, aged 35, departed in the ship " Lyon " from Plymouth, in the ship " William and Elizabeth," of which he was commander. " The Lyon " was bound for Virginia. (CARRION *v.* HAMILTON.)

In the Public Record Office, London.

CHANCERY PROCEEDINGS BEFORE 1714.

REYN. 443/77.

PERRY *v.* BATHURST.

1704/5, Feb. 9.

PERRY, Micajah, and partners complain that in 1693 they employed

BATHURST, Edward, as their Agent, and sent him in the " Little Baltemore,"

WHARTON, Thomas, commander, to Maryland.

DUNKLEY, Robert, of London, merchant, a partner.

Action for an account.

In the Public Record Office, London.

CHANCERY PROCEEDINGS.

C. 9. 183/40 AND 291/43.

FORD *v.* PENN

and

PENN *v.* FORD.

1705, Oct.

PENN, William, of Worminghurst, Essex, on 23 Aug. 1682, went from London to Deal to embark for Pennsylvania. Conveyed lands there in 1690 to Philip FORD, of London, his agent, late master of a small school.

CARPENTER, Samuel, his house in Philadelphia, 1690.

FORD, Philip, treasurer of "The Free Society of Traders in Pennsylvania," his will 20 Jan. 1699/1700 refers to purchase of lands there and in Philadelphia. His eldest dau. Bridget (m. James AYRAY), his son Philip, his daurs. Ann and Susannah. Bridget FORD, the relict, proved the will in 1705. (P.C.C. 199 GEE.)

In the Public Record Office, London.

CHANCERY PROCEEDINGS BEFORE 1714.

COLLINS 345.

DOYLEY *v.* PERRY.

1706, May 8.

DOYLEY, Robert, clerk, rector of Margaret Roding, Essex, his brother

DOYLEY, Cope, rector of Williamsberg, Virginia, died possessed of property, slaves, etc., and had dealings with

PERRY, Micajah and Richard, of London, merchants, partners with

LANE, Thomas.

DOYLEY, Charles, eldest son, aged 12, and Cope, aged 6, are sons of the said Cope.

HARRISON, Benjamin, who lives in Virginia, combines with the PERRYS and refuses to come to an account.

In the Public Record Office, London.

CHANCERY PROCEEDINGS.

C. 24. 1277. PT. 2. 23.

1707, May 8.

CHECKLEY, Samuel, of Boston, New England, chirurgeon, aged 45, now lodging at the widow ALEXANDER's on Tower Hill, deposes as to ship " Reward."

DUDLEY, Thomas, was master on her last voyage from Boston to London.

List of people in Boston to whom money was paid for refitting the ship. (DUDLEY v. OVERTON.)

In the Public Record Office, London.

CHANCERY BILLS AND ANSWERS BEFORE 1714.

REYN. 188/70.

PERRY v. MINGE.

1707, May 11.

PERRY, Micajah, and partners, complain that

BRIDGER, Col. Samuel, and

GODWIN, Edmond, of Virginia, merchants, employed them as Agents, and in 1704 consigned " The Nicholson," 100 tons,

PAIN, Ebenezer, master, and

MINGE, Robert, mate, afterwards master.

SPARROW, George, subsequently master.

Action against MINGE for an account.

In the Principal Probate Registry, London.

P.C.C. ADMON. ACT BOOK, 1707.

1707, Aug. 7.

HARVEY, Thomas, a bachelor, of H.M. ship " Deptford." Administration to

ALLAWAY, Rebecca, wife of Abraham, now at Boston, New England, a creditor.

In the Public Record Office, London.

EXCHEQUER DEPOSITIONS.

7 ANNE, EASTER 10.

1708, April 12.

BUCK, George, son of Hartwell B., *versus*
FURZE, Samuel, and Sarah his wife.
Ship called "The Happy Return" of Bideford; voyage to Maryland.
TRACY, John, and wife Sarah, parents of deft. Sarah.

In the Principal Probate Registry, London.

P.C.C. 88 LEEDS.

1708, June 24.

PERRY, John, of Antigua in America, but now of S^t. James, Westminster, merchant, his will. "Youghal, where I was born." Mary, widow of my brother Samuel; my nephew Saml.; my daus. Ann, Dorothy and $Eliz^{th}$; my nephew Jonathan, son of Edwd.
OSBOURNE, Ann, widow, my sister, her daughters Joyce O., and MILLS, Mary.
FREEMAN, Jo, son of James, and grandson of said Ann OSBOURNE.
PERRY, Mary, my dau., my plantation in South Carolina.
Admon. 4 April, 1713.

In the Public Record Office, London.

CHANCERY PROCEEDINGS.

C. 29. 1301/63.

1709/10, March 11.

NEWBURY, Walter, of Boston, New England, merchant, aged 27, lodging at Mr. WYATT'S, a haberdasher, at "The Crown," Grace street, London, deposes. (WHATTON *v.* ALLEN.)

In the Public Record Office, London.

CHANCERY BILLS AND ANSWERS BEFORE 1714.

COLLINS 409/70.

FREEMAN *v.* PERRY.

1711/12, Jan. 18.
FREEMAN, Robert, and Margery his wife, sister of
NASON, John, decd., who lived in Virginia, leaving a widow
NASON, Katherine, who with
WALKER, Col. John, were his executors.
WISE, Robert, and
LEE, Richard, are concerned.
PERRY, Micajah, answers the FREEMAN's bill of complaint.

In the Public Record Office, London.

CHANCERY BILLS AND ANSWERS BEFORE 1714.

HAM. 202/62.

LANGLEY *v.* GUNTON.

1712, July.
LANGLEY, Peter, of Woodberry, Devon, shipwright, and Elizabeth his wife.
MARCH, Elizabeth, now of Woodberry, widow, late of Charles Town in New England, and Matthew M., her son, now of St. Paul's, Shadwell, Middx., weaver, late of Charles Town, *versus*
GUNTON, Samuel, and
PICKERING, John, and Sarah his wife.
  Concerning the estate of Nathaniel GUNTON of East Ham, Essex, deceased, brother of the said Elizabeth MARCH; Matthew MARCH and Elizabeth LANGLEY being her children.

In the Public Record Office, London.

CHANCERY PROCEEDINGS, 1714-58.

BUNDLE 292. PERRY *v.* CUSTIS.

1712/3, March 14.

CUSTIS, John, jun^r., and Frances his wife, and
BIRD, William, and Lucy his wife, answer complaint of
PERRY, Micajah and Richard, reciting that
PARKE, Col. Daniel, descd., was seized of the parsonage of Whitchurch, Hants, etc., made his will 1709, died at S^t. John's, Antigua, leaving to Frances CUSTIS his dau. his estates in Virginia and England, his heirs calling themselves PARKE; remainder to
BIRD, Lucy, his dau. and to the heirs of
CHESTER, Mrs. Catherine, his youngest dau., remainder to the heirs of
PARKE, Julius Cæsar, and made the compl^{ts}. and
LANE, Thomas, his executors.

In the Public Record Office, London.

CHANCERY : TOWN DEPOSITIONS.

C. 24. 1331, 54.

1713/4, Jan. 4, etc.

WAKEFIELD, Obadiah, of New England, master of the "Prince Eugene," now in Church Hole in the Thames, aged 33.
HILTON, Robert, late of New England, merchant, aged 50, now lodging at the house of Alexander HOLMES in Duke's Place, Aldgate.
WATERS, Thomas, of Salem in New England, mariner, aged 49, now lodging at the "Duke of Marlborough's Head," Fox's lane, Shadwell.

In the Public Record Office, London.

EXCHEQUER DEPOSITIONS.

1 GEO. I, MICH. 37.

1714, Nov. 16.
Freight of the brigantine "Providence" from Liverpool to New York (*see also* 1 Geo. I, Hil. 20, and Easter 21.)
CUNINGHAM, John, merchant,
PEARSON, Joseph, mariner, *versus*
BOOTH, Anthony,
WHITESIDE, John,
DAWSON, James,
LEECH, Edward,
BROWN, John,
COORE, Thomas,
HEWETT, Richard,
TUITTE, Robert,
OLDFIELD, John,
MOORE, Andrew,
CLAYTON, Wm.,
ALLOTT, Wm.,
GILDART, Richard,
POOLE, Edward,
HALL, Peter.

In the Public Record Office, London.

CHANCERY PROCEEDINGS 1714-58.

BUNDLE 2286.   SHERRARD *v.* PERRY.

1714, Nov. 29.
SHERRARD, D[r]. William, residing at Smyrna, complains that in 1700 he with
PARKE, Colonel Daniel (died in 1710),
SHERMAN, John, and
HALLETT, Sir James, invested in a cargo from London to Virginia, consigned to
SHERRARD, Samuel, or Sampson, then residing in Virginia.
PERRY, Micajah and Richard, of London, merchants, executors of
PARKE.

In the Public Record Office, London.

CHANCERY PROCEEDINGS.

C. 24. 1342/58.

1715, April 27.
DRY, William, of Charles Town, South Carolina, aged 22, now lodging at the Marine Coffee House, Birchin lane, London, deposes that he was born and bred there (Charles Town) and served apprentice to a merchant there for seven years. (STOCKDALE *v.* GODIN.)

In the Public Record Office, London.

CHANCERY PROCEEDINGS.

C. 24. 1354/67.

WILCOCKS *v.* PAGE.

1716, June 21.
WEEKS, Elizabeth, wife of Francis, of Virginia, merchant, now lodging at the house of the *defendant* WILCOCKS at Harrow on the Hill, Middlesex, deposes.

In the Public Record Office, London.

CHANCERY PROCEEDINGS 1714–58.

BUNDLE 967. LLOYD *v.* PERRY.

1716, Oct. 1.
LLOYD, John, of Bachecrick, Denbigh, Esq., seized of land in Richmond, Virginia, dwelt there for several years, returned to England in 1694 leaving plantations in care of
LLOYD, Thomas. his brother. Action for an account.

In the Public Record Office, London.

CHANCERY PROCEEDINGS.

C. 24. 1360/46.

1717, May.
ALLEN, Eleazar, merchant, aged 25, of South Carolina, now resident at Mr. HARRISON, a watchmaker's house, in Burchen lane, London, deposes. (NEVAROS *v.* CRAVEN.)

In the Public Record Office, London.

CHANCERY PROCEEDINGS 1714-58.

BUNDLE 2287. WILLIS *v.* PERRY.

1718, Nov. 18.
WILLIS, Francis, of London, merchant, complains that PERRY, Micajah, of London, merchant, assured him that LLOYD, John, of Bachecricke, Denbigh, Esq., was seized of lands in Farnham, Richmond, Virginia, and of lands called Marguicicke, Gumfield and Great Fort.
Action for damages.

In the Principal Probate Registry, London.

P.C.C. ADMONS. 1719.

1719, Oct. 19.
HARVEY, Peter, a bachelor, died in New England. Administration to DAVIS, Joseph, a creditor.
OAKLEY, Deborah, widow, his sister renouncing.

In the Public Record Office, London.

CHANCERY PROCEEDINGS 1714–58.

BUNDLE 767. CARRUTHERS v. PERRY.

1719, Oct. 21.
CARRUTHERS, Robert, of London, merchant, complains that
WILSON, Willis, of Virginia, gent., by his will 1706, gave to
HALBERT, Lucy, dau. of Lucy H., of Deptford, Kent, widow, £50.
WILSON, Jane, Col. William, and Samuel,
LEIGH, Col. William, and
WALLACE, James, executors, all of Virginia, merchants,
HOOKE, Martha, then partner of Lucy HALBERT, the mother,
HANSON, Malon, of Lymehouse, carpenter, married Lucy H., dau.,
PERRY, Micajah and Richard, merchants, are defendants.

In the Public Record Office, London.

EXCHEQUER DEPOSITIONS.

7 GEO. I. HIL. 10.

1720, Aug. 4.
Depositions at New York.
SUMMERS, Thomas,
HALSALL, James,
MARTINDALE, John, versus,
FOSTER, Benjamin,
CHESHIRE, William,
DITCHFIELD, Thomas.
Ship called "The Good Intent," pink of Liverpool.

Rev. T. Dickenson's Nonconformist Register of Northowram, Yorks.

1721/2. Feb. 1.
FOSTER, Mr. Benjn., my Bro, and
VANINGBRO, Mrs. Hannah, mar. at New York.

In the Guildhall Library, London.

NAYLER'S PRIVATE ACTS OF PARLIAMENT.

9/6.

A.D.
c. 1724. TAYLOR, Maria, dau. of Thos., of Kensington, Middx. (*ob.* 1716), marr. 1724 W^m. BYRD and had issue William, Anne, m. CARTER, Charles, now in Virginia, and Maria, married CARTER, Landon, and had an only child, Maria.

In the Principal Probate Registry, London.

P.C.C. 124 GREENLY.

A.D.
1726. PARKER, John, of Thornbury, Glouc., yeoman, in his will names BRENTON, John, William and Jane, of Birmingham, Pensylvania.

In the Public Record Office, London.

EXCHEQUER DEPOSITIONS.

5 GEO. II. MICH. 27.

1731, Oct. 22.
JEFFERYS, Herbert, gent., *versus*
LEWIS, Edward, gent., and Thos.
THOMAS, James and Thos.
MATTHEWS, Henry, and Mary his wife.
EDWARDS, Thomas, of S^t. Anne, Essex, Virginia, clerk, deceased, his estate in Kington, Hereford.
RICKARDS, John, Peter and Robert, Esq^{rs}., mentioned.

In the Public Record Office, London.

EXCHEQUER DEPOSITIONS.

7 GEO. II. EASTER 10.

1734, May 12.
Depositions taken at Boston, Mass.
LUSCOMBE, Nicholas, and Joanna his wife, admrix of
HURRELL, Roger, late of Woodley, Devon, *versus*
HURRELL, John, gent., Roger, of Charleton, Richard, and
HURRELL, Thomas, clerk.
(*See also* 7 Geo. II. Mich. 24.)

In H.M. General Register House, Edinburgh.

COMM. COURT OF EDINBURGH.

1738, May 25.
LAING, William, of Freehold, co. Monmouth, New Jersey, died
——. Inventory by W^m. CHALMERS (?) Writer (?) in Edinburgh, husband of Barbara, dau. of George LAING, deceased, merchant in Old Aberdeen, the brother-german. Debt due from James LAING in Kirktown of Fetter Angus, son of George LAING in Longside, brother of said William, an " oecnymist " in King's College in Aberdeen in 1685.

In the Principal Probate Registry, London.

P.C.C. 16 GREENLY.

A.D.
1738. HAMMERTON, Elizabeth, of Charlestown, South Carolina, widow, in her will names Hollier HAMMERTON,
HOLLIER, Nathaniel, of Lynn, Norfolk,
BRASSEUR, Ann de la,
BARRY, Joseph,
BEAUCHAMP, Adam, and others.

In H.M. General Register House, Edinburgh.

COMM. EDINBURGH.

1739, Jan. 9.
SCOTT, M^r. Alexander, rector of Overworl, county Stafford, on river Potomack, Virginia, died 1 April, 1738. Inventory by George SCOTT, writer in Edinburgh, the brother german.

In the Public Record Office, London.

CHANCERY PROCEEDINGS, 1714–58.

BUNDLE 1591. PERRY *v.* BRADLEY.

1740, Nov. 21.
PERRY, William, of Wolverhampton, Staffs., bucklemaker, and Mary his wife, complain that Mary being a dau. of
MARSH, Nathan, flaxdresser, deceased, and Mary his wife, Mary her grandmother was seized of premises in Oaken, parish of Codsall, and died in 1733. John her husband died in 1734.
PEARSEHOUSE, Sarah, now wife of Benjamin, sister of Mary PERRY.
BRADLEY, Samuel, of Dudley, Worc., collier, married Phebe MARSH, sister of said Nathan.
BATCH, Peter, who lived in Virginia, brother to plaintiff Mary's grandmother, had no lawful issue, but his son Alexander assigned the premises to one
HOPKINS . . . Samuel BRADLEY answers.

In the Principal Probate Registry, London.

P.C.C. ADMONS.

1741/2, Jan. 8.
WILLS, George, of New England in parts beyond the seas, but died on H.M.S. "Drayton," in H.M's service. Admin. to Alex^r. WATT, attorney, of Mary WILLS, the relict, now residing in New England.

In the Principal Probate Registry, London.

P.C.C. ADMONS.

1742, Sept. 15.

ROBERTS, John, late of Philadelphia, North America, and belonging to the merchant ship "Alexander," but in S^t. Thomas Hospital, Southwark, Surrey. Admon. to W^m. PLAYTER, attorney of Grace ROBERTS, widow, the relict, residing at Philadelphia.

In the Public Record Office, London.

CHANCERY PROCEEDINGS 1758-1800 (*sic*).

BUNDLE 1767. DUNN *v.* PERRY.

1742/3, Feb. 1.

DUNN, Samuel, of Rotherhithe, Surrey, joyner, and Adriana his wife, late

OAKLEY, Adriana, widow, complain that

HARDING, William, of S^t. Mary, Rotherhithe, mariner, in 1739 by will gave apparel to his brother Philip H. Was in the service as Captain of his ships of

HANBURY, John, merchant of London.

In 1741 HARDING went to Virginia to take command of the "Dunkirk," but died there 28 Aug. 1742. HANBURY combines with

PERRY, Elizabeth, and others to obstruct the execution of HARDING'S will.

In the Principal Probate Registry, London.

P.C.C. 313 GREENLY.

A.D.

1743. ANNELY, Richard, of New York, merchant, in his will names Thomas, Elizabeth and Susannah ANNELY.

BOURDETT, Judith and Samuel.

JENKINS, Walter, of Bristol.

In the Principal Probate Registry, London.

P.C.C. 44 GREENLY.

A.D.

743. GREEN, John, of Boston, New England, merchant, and of London, in his will names Joseph and Benjamin GREEN.
KILBY, Christopher.
SEDGWICK, Rebecca.
HULL, Judith and Ann.
LEIGH, Richard.

In the Public Record Office, London.

CHANCERY PROCEEDINGS, 1714–58.

BUNDLE 1844. PERRY *v.* HOPKINS.

1744, May 23.
HOPKINS, James, answers complaint of
PERRY, William, and Mary his wife, reciting that
BACH, Alexander, eldest son and heir of Peter, of Oaken in Codsall, was, in 1732, of Hanover, Prince William co., Virginia, planter, conveyed premises to
HOPKINS, William, of the Middle Temple, London, gent., then of Williamsburg, Virginia, who died, leaving
BARRADAILE, Edward, Esq., late Attorney General in Virginia, his sole devisee and executor.
MARSH, Mary (*née* BACH), in 1722, took possession; John of Over Penn, Stafford, tailor, her husband; Nathan MARSH their son, was father of complt. Mary PERRY.
PERSEHOUSE, Sarah, wife of Benjn., and
SHARPLES, Phebe, wife of John, were daughters of Nathan MARSH.
BRADLEY, Phebe, wife of Samuel, was eldest daughter of John MARSH.

In the Public Record Office, London.

CHANCERY PROCEEDINGS, 1714–58.

BUNDLE 2268, LOWRY *v.* PERRY.

1744, May 25.

LOWRY, John, of South Benfleet, Essex, yeoman, complains that his father John (died July, 1721), of the same place, was agent to
HAMMOND, Margaret, relict of Henry, of S^t. Katherine by the Tower, who died intestate in Oct. 1724. W^m. H., their son, died and left a will 12 July, 1732, mentioning his uncle
CLOPTON, William, and made
SKINNER, Samuel, of Stepney, gent., and
COLE, Josiah, of Mark Lane, M.D., his executors.

William CLOPTON and his children are planters in Virginia.
PERRY, Micajah, of S^t. Mary Axe, London, a deft., states that
CLOPTON, Robert and Walter,
MILLS, Nic., and
MOSS, Alexander, were the children of William CLOPTON.
HAMMOND, Henry, in his will names the children of his wife's brother,
CLOPTON, William, Anne, wife of Nic. MILLS, and Elizth., wife of Alex^r. Moss.

In the Public Record Office, London.

CHANCERY PROCEEDINGS, 1714–58.

BUNDLE 2108. SAVAGE *v.* PERRY.

1745, Nov. 27.

SAVAGE, William, of Imworth, Essex, only son of Edward, of Hanvill, Essex, son of Edward, of Hanvill, uncle of
HAMMOND, Henry, of London, citizen and clothworker, deceased, who by will left property to his wife's brother
CLOPTON, William, living in Virginia; he is now dead leaving four children, Robert, Walter,
MILLS, Ann, wife of Nic, and
MOSS, Elizabeth, wife of Alexander, who have always lived in Virginia.

In the Principal Probate Registry, London.

P.C.C. 330 GREENLY.

A.D.
1745. JENYS, Thomas, of Charles Town, South Carolina, merchant, in his will mentions Paul and George JENYS.
BRIAN, Hugh.
OSLER, Mary.
PINCKNEY, Charles.
RUTLIDGE, Andrew.
BASNETT, John.
GIBBES, Elizabeth.
EVANCE, Branfill.
BEDON, Stephen & Jos.
EDGAR, Edward.
DALE, Thomas.

Registers of St. George's Chapel, Hyde Park Corner, Middx.

1745/6, Jan. 11.
DYMOND, M^r. George, and
WILLIS, Mrs. Abigail, of Boston in New England, married.

1745/6, Jan. 20,
DYMOND, Sarah, d^r. of George & Abigail, from Boston in New England, baptized.

In the Principal Probate Registry, London.

P.C.C. 146 GREENLY.

A.D.
1746. DUKINFIELD, Nathaniel, of Uckinton, Cheshire, Esq., in his will mentions estate in North Carolina and names Margaret, Samuel & John DUKINFIELD,
CHORLEY, Jane & John,
COLLET, Joseph,
BIER, William, and
POTTS, Dorothy.

In the Public Record Office, London.

CHANCERY PROCEEDINGS 1714–58.

BUNDLE 1449. BENNETT *v.* PERRY.

1747, Sept. 21.
BENNETT, Richard, of Wye, Maryland, merchant, complains that, owning a tobacco estate in Maryland, he consigned tobacco to PERRY, Micajah, & Philip, merchants in London, who pretend that they have paid the balance of the account.

In the Principal Probate Registry, London.

P.C.C. 51 GREENLY.

A.D.
1747. MACKINTOSH, Charles, of New York, in his will names Phineas, Susanna and Alexander MACKINTOSH.
BAYARD, Stephen.
ALSOP, Richard.
PARKER, Elisha.
FOLL, Susanna & John, 1749.

In the Principal Probate Registry, London.

P.C.C. 160 GREENLY.

A.D.
1747. WALL, Mary, of Goswell street, London, grocer, in her will names Elizabeth & Henry WALL of Maryland, America.

In the Principal Probate Registry, London.

P.C.C. 219 GREENLY.

A.D.
1747. YEAMANS, John, of S^t. James's, Westminster, Esq., in his will mentions
DE WINDT, Johannis, of S^t. Thomas, America,
STODDARD, Elizabeth, of Boston, New England, Mary, Sarah and Mehitabel STODDARD, and
HUTCHINSON, Eliakim, of Boston.

In the Parish Register of Gulval, Cornwall.

1748, Dec. 20.
ROBERTSON, Samuel, of Philadelphia, and
WATTS, Phillis, married.

In the Principal Probate Registry, London.

P.C.C. 285 GREENLY.

A.D.
1748. BAYLISS, Featherston, of Frederica, Georgia, surgeon, in his will mentions
BELLINGHURST, Mrs. Anne.
MOLLEY, Featherston & Francis, of Piccadilly.
DAWSON, Elizabeth & Matthew, of Newcastle-on-Tyne.
HORTON, Major William.
McKEY, Capt. James.
GOLDSMITH, Lieut. Thomas.
GODIN, David.
SPUTLEDGE, Andrew.
CAMPBELL, James.

In the Principal Probate Registry, London.

P.C.C. 8 GREENLY.

A.D.
1748. DICKSON, Thomas, of H.M.S. "Worcester," surgeon, in his will names
GARDINER, Silvester, of Boston in New England, physician.

In the Principal Probate Registry, London.

P.C.C. 118 GREENLY.

A.D.
1748. ILES, Joseph, of Bristol, merchant, in his will names
SAVAGE, Benjamin, John & Jeremiah, of Carolina.

In the Principal Probate Registry, London.

P.C.C. 85 GREENLY.

A.D.
1748. MODYFORD, Ann, of New Windsor, Berks, spinster, in her will mentions her estate in Jamaica & America and names
MESSENGER, Mary.
GLADIN, Richard.
JONES, Elizabeth & Bridget.
BOWLES, M^r. Norton, Ann & Charles.
SMITH, Dorothy.
BLAKE, John.
STAPLES, Thomas.

In the Principal Probate Registry, London.

P.C.C. 243 GREENLY.

A.D.
1748. SINCLAIR, George, in his will of this date mentions Elizabeth
SINCLAIR of Delaval, Philadelphia.
LLOYD, Capt. John.
BAILEY, Edward.
HOOTON, Thomas, and
ROBERTS, Robert.

*From the MSS. of J. R. Carr-Ellison, Esq.,
at Dunston Hill, Newcastle-on-Tyne.*

(HIST. MSS. COMMISSION, 15TH REPORT, APP. X. 92.)

A.D.
1748. At Boston.
WENDELL, Messrs.,
INMAN, Ralph,
QUINCY, Edmund, Henry & Josiah,
HUTCHINSON, Thomas,
BOWDOIN, William,
WENTWORTH, Samuel, and
DOUGLAS, Samuel, correspond with
CARR, Ralph, of Newcastle, merchant & banker.

In the Principal Probate Registry, London.

P.C.C. 65 GREENLY.

A.D.
1748. WOODBRIDGE, Ruth, of Boston, "lately of the Barbadoes," in
her will names
HAGGETT, Susannah, Jane, Nathaniel & William.
ALLEYNE, Mary.
WILLSHIRE, Col. Richard & Thomas.
BOWDEINE, William.
HANNEN, Jos.

*From the MSS. of J. R. Carr-Ellison, Esq.,
at Dunston Hill, Newcastle-on-Tyne.*

(HIST. MSS. COMMISSION, 15TH REPORT, APP. X. 92.)

A.D.
1749. At New York.
COMMELIN, Robert,
BARD, John,
BRINKERHOFF, Joris,
SCHUYLER, Adoniah,
CUYLER, Henry,
WATTS, John,
LANE, Henry, and
LIVINGSTON, Philip, correspond with
CARR, Ralph, of Newcastle, merchant & banker.

In the Principal Probate Registry, London.

P.C.C. 264 GREENLY.

A.D.
1749. GRIFFIN, Lucock, of Kingston, Jamaica, Esq., in his will names
Mary, Henrietta & John Giles GRIFFIN of Philadelphia,
MANNING, Hon. Edward,
HUME, Hon. Benjamin,
VALLETTE, Hon. Peter, and others.

In the Principal Probate Registry, London.

P.C.C. 198 GREENLY.

A.D.
1749. GRONOUS, Elizabeth, of S^t. Clement Danes, Middx., spinster, in
her will mentions
PROBART, William, of Pecembe river, Worcester, Virginia, and
Frances PROBART.

In the Principal Probate Registry, London.

P.C.C. ADMONS. 1750.

1750, Dec. 14.
HARVEY, Nicholas, a bachelor, Lieutenant in the Independent Company of Foot, commanded by CLARKE, Captain, at Albany, New York. Administration to HARVEY, Rev. Peter, the brother ; Jane H., the mother renouncing.

In the Principal Probate Registry, London.

P.C.C. 289 GREENLY.

A.D.
1750. COWLINGTON, William, citizen and pewterer of London, and of Jamaica, in his will mentions TRECOTHICK. Barlow, of Boston, New England.

In the Guildhall Library, London.

NAYLER'S PRIVATE ACTS OF PARLIAMENT.

VOL. 5/3 & 4.

A.D.
1750. JEKYLL, John, of New England, had issue Thomas.
John, of New England, married Margaret & had a son, John, born 1738 in New England.

In the Principal Probate Registry, London.

P.C.C. 396 GREENLY.

A.D.
1750. PILGRIM, Robert, late chief factor to the Hudson's Bay Company, "now at Hackney," Middlesex, in his will names John PILGRIM.
PELL, Robert & Martha.
HIGON, Ehua.
SOWTER, John.
CANEY, James.

In the Principal Probate Registry, London.

P.C.C. 396 GREENLY.

A.D.
c. 1750 [*but undated*].
PLAISTED, Thomas, of S^t. Mary, Islington, Middx., gent., in his will names Rebecca & Susan PLAISTED, and estate in New England.
Proved 1750.

In the Principal Probate Registry, London.

P.C.C. ADMONS.

1754, May 7.
VAUGHAN, Martha, *alias* UNDERWOOD, of South Carolina, widow, deceased. Admon. to William UNDERWOOD, the brother.

In the Principal Probate Registry, London.

P.C.C. ADMONS.

1754, July 5.
GULLIVER, Elijah, of Milton, Suffolk, Massachusetts, New England, formerly of H.M.S. " Vigilant " and " Superbe." Admon. to Henry RAINSDON, attorney of Samuel GULLIVER, the brother, now residing in the above country.

In the Principal Probate Registry, London

P.C.C. ADMONS.

1754, Aug. 14.
GRICE, Cesar, of Maryland, died " in partibus." Admon. to John GRICE, the brother, —— GRICE, the relict having died.

In the Principal Probate Registry, London.

P.C.C. ADMONS.

1754, Aug. 20.
WRIGHT, Mary, heretofore
THOROGOOD, formerly
TREVETHAN, late of Virginia, deceased. Admon. to Daniel HIGHMORE, attorney of Stephen WRIGHT, the son, now residing in Virginia.

In the Principal Probate Registry, London.

P.C.C. 134 PAUL.

1755, April 25.
HARVEY, Sarah, of S^t. George's, Hanover Square, Middx., sp^r.; her will names
HOCKLEY, Richard, in Philadelphia, merchant,
SCHUBERT, Ann & Mary, daughters of Ann, Philadelphia.
Proved 23 May, 1755.

In the Register of Marriages, Edinburgh, Scotland.

1756, Dec. 26.

BLAIR, John, jun., son to John BLAIR, councillor in Virginia, and Miss Jean, daughter to Archibald BLAIR, writer, both in the New North parish, married.

From the Annual Register for 1762.

P. 136.

A.D.

1762. KELLO, John, of Bloomsbury, Middlesex, aged 26, came from Virginia, son of a merchant in Houndsditch, executed for forgery, brother of Joseph, aged 24, clerk to

MORE, Mr. Charles, of Aldermanbury, London.

In the Principal Probate Registry, London.

P.C.C. ADMONS.

1763, Aug. 5.

OGILVIE, William, Esq., late Captain in one of H.M's Independent Companies of Foot, in the Province of New York, a bachelor, deceased. Admon. to Joseph MICO, attorney of Rev. John OGILVIE, clerk, the brother, now residing at Montreal, Canada.

From the MSS. of J. R. Carr-Ellison, Esq.,

at Dunston Hill, Newcastle-on-Tyne.

(HIST. MSS. COMMISSION, 15TH REPORT, APP. X. 92.)

A.D.

1763. FLETCHER, William, a merchant, "having left Boston for the safer Danish island of S^t. Eustathia," his character was re-established, a composition was paid and correspondence resumed with

CARR, Ralph, of Newcastle, merchant and banker.

*From the MSS. of J. R. Carr-Ellison, Esq.,
at Dunston Hill, Newcastle-on-Tyne.*

(HIST. MSS. COMMISSION, 15TH REPORT, APP. X. 94.)

1764, Oct. 26.
WENTWORTH, Samuel, Esq., at Boston (d. Sept. 1766) received a letter of this date, mentioning the return of H. WENTWORTH, a son, who had given Messrs. CARR great satisfaction, and of another son at Eton, who appears to have returned home in May, 1765.
CARR, Ralph, of Newcastle, merchant & banker, the writer.

*From the MSS. of J. R. Carr-Ellison, Esq.,
at Dunston Hill, Newcastle-on-Tyne.*

(HIST. MSS. COMMISSION, 15TH REPORT, APP. X. 92.)

A.D.
1764. At New York.
FRANKLIN, Walter & Samuel,
BOMPER, Lodowick,
VARDILL, Thomas, and
SARLY, Jacob, correspond with
CARR, Ralph, of Newcastle, merchant & banker.

*From the MSS. of J. R. Carr-Ellison, Esq.,
at Dunston Hill, Newcastle-on-Tyne.*

(HIST. MSS. COMMISSION, 15TH REPORT, APP. X. 92.)

A.D.
1764. At Boston.
GOULD, John,
BETHUNE, Nath. & George,
SCOLLAY, Samuel,
OLIVER, Hon. Andrew, and
GRIFFIN, James, correspond with
CARR, Ralph, of Newcastle, merchant & banker.

From the MSS. of J. R. Carr-Ellison, Esq.,

at Dunston Hill, Newcastle-on-Tyne.

(HIST. MSS. COMMISSION, 15TH REPORT, APP. X. 95.)

1765, July 23.
 DUNBAR, M^r. William, of Thurso in Caithness, " the son of a very reputable clergyman," is strongly recommended for employment on going out to New York, by
 CARR, Ralph, of Newcastle, merchant and banker.

From the Papers of the Earl of Dartmouth,

Patshull, Stafford, 1874.

(HIST. MSS. COMMISSION., 2ND REPORT, APP., P. 12.)

A.D.
1765. SMITH, William, of New York, letter to
 WHITFIELD, Rev^d. M^r., on the discontents in America, specially regarding the Stamp Act.

A.D.
1773-5. REED, Judith, of Philadelphia, letters from, touching the rebellion.

From the Annual Register for 1766, *p.* 183.

NARRATIVE OF CAPTAIN HARRISON.

A.D.
1766. HARRISON, Captain David, of " The Peggy," of New York.
 CAMPBELL, James, mariner, died raving mad.
 FLAT, David, a foremast man, upon whom the lot fell to be killed and eaten.
 DOUD, James, mate, died during the voyage.
 EVERS, Captain Thomas, of " The Susannah " of London, in the Virginia trade.
 WARNER, . . . a seaman, died during the voyage.
 ASHLEY, Lemuel, a seaman.
 WENTWORTH, Samuel, a seaman.

From the Annual Register for 1767.

PAGE 211.

A.D.
1767. TABRY, Anthony, master of the brig " Sally," bound from Philadelphia to Hispaniola. An account of the sufferings of the crew.
MARS, Humphry, mate.
SHERVER, Joseph, mariner.
BESS, Samuel, mariner.
BURNA, John, mariner.
TOY, Peter, mariner.
CULTAIN, Daniel, mariner.
DAVIS, John, mariner.
LANDERRY, Alexander, mariner.
MAYES, Peter, mariner.
HAMMON, William, mariner.
NOYES, Capt. Robert, of the brig " Norwich."

In Marcham's Rough List of Deeds, 1910.

LOT 25.

1768, Apl. 22.
IZARD, Rebecca, spinster, younger dau. of Ralph, late of the province of South Carolina, and Colin CAMPBELL of Berner Street, Marylebone, Middx. Articles of marriage.
BLAKE, Daniel, of South Carolina, a party.
ARGYLE, John, Duke of, a party,
CAMPBELL, Hon. W^m., his younger son, a party.

*From the MSS. of J. R. Carr-Ellison, Esq.,
at Dunston Hill, Newcastle-on-Tyne.*

(HIST. MSS. COMMISSION, 15TH REPORT, APP. X. 95.)

1768, April 29.
    INMAN, M^r. Ralph, is requested to make quest for "a very unfortunate poor lady at Roxbury."
    HESILRIGE, Lady, wife of the son [Robert] of Sir Arthur H., who is enquired for by
    ORMSTON, M^r. Jonathan, Sir Arthur's trustee. Also for
    NICHOLSON, Hannah, of Newcastle, a poor woman, who has never received a legacy of £200 left her in 1763 by her son Edward N., in Virginia, and retained by
    HUNTER, James, there. He of Fredericksburgh, Virginia, in a letter of 2 July, 1770.

In the Register of Marriages, Edinburgh, Scotland.

1768, Aug. 7.
    BARCLAY, David, merchant, of Waterlane, London, and
    DAY, M^{rs}. Janet, late of Boston in New England, widow, both in New North Kirk parish, married.

From the Marriage Registers of Edinburgh, Scotland.

1769, March 12.
    KEITH, William, eldest son of D^r. William KEITH of South Carolina, and
    MOODIE, Miss Jean, d. of James M. of Jamaica, both in New Kirk parish, married.

From the Marriage Registers of Edinburgh, Scotland.

1770, Nov. 24.
THOMSON, Alexander (son to James THOMSON, accountant in the Excise Office) in Savannah in the Province of Georgia, married to
SPENCER, Mary Elisabeth, d. of William SPENCER, collector of H.M. Customs of said port ; mar. by Rev. M^r. Samuel FRINK, rector of the parish of Christ Church there.

In the Principal Probate Registry, London.

P.C.C. ADMONS.

1772, Jan. 7.
CRAVEN, Lawrence, of H.M.S. "New York," but died at Baltimore in the province of Maryland, a bachelor. Admon. to Thomas CRAVEN the brother. (Admon. *de bonis non* in March, 1778.

In the Register of Marriages, Edinburgh, Scotland.

1772, March 15.
BAKER, James Fowler, of Charlistown, South Carolina, student of physick at the University of Edinburgh, and
PRINGLE, Miss Ann, daughter of deceast Francis PRINGLE, Lieut. in the Royal American Regiment, commanded by General AMHERST, now residing in the College Kirk p. [? Parish or precinct.]

In the Principal Probate Registry, London.

P.C.C. 267 STEVENS.

1773, May 27.
SHERWOOD, Joseph, of Warnford Court, Throckmorton street, London, gentleman, in a codicil to his will names
GREENHILL, Joseph, of New England, merchant, deceased, his estate at Warbois in Huntingdonshire.

In the Parish Register of Falmouth, Cornwall.

1775, April 6.
BEEKMAN, Gerard C., of New York in North America, and
RUSSELL, Ann, married, by licence.

In the Principal Probate Registry, London.

P.C.C. 374 COLLINS.

1778, March 3.
PERRY, Richard, of S^t. Mary Whitechapel, Middx., his will names Benjamin, my only son.
SAVAGE, Elizabeth Marshall, "my only dau.," of Philadelphia, America.
Proved 19 July, 1780.

In the Principal Probate Registry, London.

P.C.C. 57 COLLINS.

1778, Oct. 26.

BURNLEY, John, of Hanover County, York river, Virginia, his will names his brothers Zachariah BURNLEY, Hardin & Richard.
DUKE, Elizabeth, my sister, and her children.
DUKE, Keziah, my sister, and her children.
LITTLEPAGE, Ann, my sister, wife of Thomas L.
MEREWEATHER, Judith, my sister, late wife of James M., & her sons David, James & William.
ELSWORTH, George, my prentice.

In the Principal Probate Registry, London.

P.C.C. 361 CORNWALLIS.

1779, June 9.

HARVEY, Margaret, of S^t. Paul, Covent Garden, Middx., spinster, in her will names
WINDUS, Ann, my sister, deceased.
WINDUS, Dymoke, my nephew, "supposed to b͡ in America," and other relatives.
Proved 18 July, 1783.

In the Principal Probate Registry, London.

P.C.C. ADMONS. 1782.

1782, Dec. 24.

HARVEY, Stephen, Esq., of Saratoga, North America, a bachelor, Lieutenant in the 62nd Regiment. Administration to Eliab HARVEY, his brother.

In H.M. General Register House, Edinburgh.

COMMISSARY OF EDINBURGH.

1783, June 17.

GILLES, Robert, Captain in a Provincial Corps in H.M's Service in America (where he died). Inventory by D^r. John GILLES, presently at Lausanne, & by Colin GILLES, now in India, brothers of the deceased.

REID, James, late at Croft Creek, North Carolina, but now in Scotland, a debtor.

In H.M. General Register House, Edinburgh.

COMM. COURT OF EDINBURGH.

1783, June 26.

BALFOUR, John, sometime planter in Pedee River, South Carolina, died abroad, second son of Andrew BALFOUR, deceased, late of Braidwood, merchant in Edinburgh. Inventory by James ALEXANDER, merchant in Edinburgh, husband of Isabel, dau. of said Andrew. John B. his second son died 15 Nov. 1781 and called " eldest son " 24 Nov. 1783. Margaret ROBERTSON was wife of Andrew BALFOUR, and he had other children. Mary GRAY, widow & executor of late John BALFOUR.

In H.M. General Register House, Edinburgh.

COMM. COURT OF EDINBURGH.

1783, Sept. 1.

AITKEN, James, sometime preacher of the Gospel in Isla, thereafter in America, where he died in ——. Inventory by John AITKEN the younger of Rashie Hill, the brother. John AITKEN of Rashie Hill, cautioner.

In H.M. General Register House, Edinburgh.

COMMISSARY OF EDINBURGH.

1783, Oct. 22.

BOYD, Robert, merchant, died in Virginia, youngest son of Andrew BOYD, deceased, minister of the gospel at Twyneholm. William, minister at Pinningham, John, of Miltons, Isabel (wife of Alex^r. BROWN of Langlands), Jean (wife of John SCOTT, minister at Twyneholm), Elizabeth (wife of Henry HOLM, Writer to the Signet) are brothers and sisters german of the said Robert.

In H.M. General Register House, Edinburgh.

COMM. COURT OF EDINBURGH.

1783, Nov. 21.

WRIGHT, Alex^r. (servant to Capt. W^m. MUIR 8th [or 82nd] Foot) died at Wilmington, North America. Inventory by John WRIGHT, taylor, in Calton in Glasgow, Daniel WRIGHT, weaver there, Daniel McCOLL, schoolmaster in Glasgow, husband of Christian WRIGHT, and by Alex^r. FLEMING coalhewer at Monkland, husband of Mary WRIGHT. The said John, Daniel, Christian & Mary being brothers & sisters german of the deceased.

In H.M. General Register House, Edinburgh.

COMM. COURT OF EDINBURGH.

1784, May 27.

OGILVY, Henry, sometime shipmaster at Charlestown, S. Carolina, but died at Pensacola in West Florida in 1779. Inventory by Hannah MEADOWS, widow of Henry OGILVY the younger & for her infant child (by Henry) Harriet OGILVY. Debt after death of Catherine ROBERTSON, widow of Henry OGILVY of Templehull, who conveyed his estate to Alexander, deceased, his eldest son charged with 3000 marks to his son Henry OGILVY above, the younger 19 May, 1756; reg^d. at Dundee in 1783.

In the Principal Probate Registry, London.

P.C.C. ADMONS. 1786.

1786, Aug. 23.

HARVIE, Andrew, a servant in the Hudson's Bay Company, a bachelor, deceased at York Fort. Administration to
RUSSELL, James, attorney of
HARVEY, Andrew, his father, of Birsay, North Britain.

In the Principal Probate Registry, London.

P.C.C. ADMONS.

1787, January.

CRAWFORD, James, 1st marine H.M.S. "Raisonable," at Long Island Hospital, a widower, deceased. Admon. to James CRAWFORD, the son.

In the Principal Probate Registry, London.

P.C.C. 404 BEVOR.

1788, Jan. 9.

SCOTT, John, of Charleston, South Carolina, gentleman, son of Jonathan SCOTT, in his will names
BOWLES, Tobias,
WILLIAMS, Mrs. Elizabeth, my mother in law,
SCREVEN, Rebecca, my sister in law,
RICHARDSON, Benjamin Moodie, my godson,
WINSTANLEY, Thomas, my friend,
SCOTT, Sarah, my wife,
SMYTH, Bartlee, my nephew; Ann Harleston SMYTH and Mary Avis SMYTH, my nieces,
LANCHESTER, Mrs. Jane, and
HARLESTON, Isaac, Esq., my kinsman, named in codicil, 1789.

In the Public Record Office, London.

CHANCERY PROCEEDINGS, 1758–1800.

BUNDLE 2430, PERRY *v.* MORRISON.

1789, Feb. 27.
PERRY, James, of Wolverhampton, Staffs., merchant,
HAYES, Thomas, of Bristol, merchant, and
SHERBROOKE, Miles, of New York, merchant, complain that prior to 1775 they were partners in New York.
MORRISON, Malcolm, of the province of New York, storekeeper, gave them his land. His property confiscated by the American States. He died intestate in 1788, and Archibald his son has taken out Administration.

In the Principal Probate Registry, London.

P.C.C. ADMON. ACTS.

1789, March 14.
LYMBURNER, Matthew, formerly of S^t. Andrew's, North Brunswick, North America, but late of Penobscot, Mass. Admon. to Robert SHEDDEN, attorney of Margaret, the relict, now residing at S^t. Andrew's.

In H.M. General Register House, Edinburgh.

COMM. COURT OF EDINBURGH.

1789, May 18.
MOODIE, Jane, relict of
KEITH, D^r. William, of Charlestown, South Carolina, "at time of their death." She died at Bristol street, Edinburgh, 19 March 1789. Inventory by
MOODIE, Benjamin, Writer in Edinburgh, her brother-german.

In H.M. General Register House, Edinburgh.

COMMIS. EDINBURGH.

1790, July 5.
OGILVIE, Alexander, died in America, and James his brother, died in Gibraltar. Inventory by Isobel OGILVIE widow, in Duff, aunt by the father of above. Capt. John THOMSON (died Apl. 1778) left over £2000 to his nephews Alex^r. & James, dated 25 Apl. 1774. His sister M^{rs}. Ann THOMSON died 1786.

In the Public Record Office, London.

CHANCERY REPORTS AND CERTIFICATES.

VOL. 761.

BAKER v. HAYLEY.

1790, Dec. 7.
JEFFERY, Mary, wife of Patrick, of Boston in America, Esquire, formerly the wife, widow, relict & sole executrix of
HAYLEY, George, merchant, deceased.

In the Public Record Office, London.

CHANCERY REPORTS AND CERTIFICATES.

VOL. 761.

BLACKBURN v. FARMER.

1790, Dec. 17.
MOORE, Lewis, of Virginia, son of Lewis.
MOORE, Lewis, of New York, son of William, nephew of
MOORE, John, whose will was dated 22 July, 1780.

In the Principal Probate Registry, London.

P.C.C. ADMONS.

1791, April 5.
GRESLEY, Jeffery, late of King William County, Virginia, Esq., Admon. to Jane Grammar GRESLEY, spinster, the daughter. Mary GAINES formerly GRESLEY (wife of Robert GAINES), the relict, being cited but not appearing.

In the Principal Probate Registry, London.

P.C.C. ADMONS.

1791, April 12.
DENT, John, of Bristol, late of Bunker's Hill in North America, a bachelor, deceased. Admon. to Jane, wife of Thomas TYAS & administratrix of George DENT the brother and only next of kin.

In the Principal Probate Registry, London.

P.C.C. ADMONS.

1791, May 4.
LOGAN, Margaret, of South Carolina, in North America. Admon. to William LOGAN, the husband.

In the Principal Probate Registry, London.

P.C.C. ADMONS.

1791, May 11.
BROWN, Peter, formerly of East Florida, but late of New Providence, Bahama Islands, deceased. Admon. to James PHYN, attorney of Sarah BROWN, widow, the relict, now residing at New Providence.

In the Public Record Office, London.

EXCHEQUER DEPOSITIONS.

32 GEO. III. EASTER 12.

A.D.
1792. BELCHER, Elijah, of Savannah, Georgia, mariner, aged 17, deposes in "ANDERSON *v.* QUAYLE."

In the Principal Probate Registry, London.

P.C.C. ADMONS.

1794, Jan. 4.
ELAM, Joseph, late of Philadelphia, a bachelor, deceased. Admon. to Emanuel ELAM, the brother.

In the Principal Probate Registry, London.

P.C.C. 758 LOVEDAY.

1794, Feb. 28.
HARVEY, Mungo, of Washington, Westmoreland [Virginia] his will names
HARVEY, James, " my son," land purchased of
BALL, Ric., of Lancaster, deceased.
HARVEY, John, " my son," land on which I reside, purchased of
SILTON, John.
HARVEY, Ann, Sarah & Eliza, my daughters.
Fox, Joseph ⎫ witnesses.
LENDRUM, Thomas ⎭
Administration 31 Oct. 1809 to
MURDOCK, William, Esq., attorney of James HARVEY, the surviving executor, " now at Westmoreland."

— 98 —

In the Principal Probate Registry, London.

P.C.C. 108 EXETER.

1797, Feb. 20 (proved).
PARRY, John, of Gray's Inn, now of Kentish Town, Middx., gent., his will.
SUMMERS, John, of Stowe, near Charlestown, planter, owes £500.
FROST, Rev^d. Thomas, of Charlestown, my wife Mary's son in law.
TOWNES, M^r. Rich., decd., his estate in America; my wife's former husband, their ch^n. Elizth., wife of Thos. FROST, and
SMITH, Ann, wife of Charles SMITH, jun^r., of Charlestown, Esq.
FROST, Elizth., the said, went out to Charlestown Xmas 1786. Charlestown, the place of my wife's nativity.

In the Public Record Office, London.

CHANCERY PROCEEDINGS, 1758-1800.

BUNDLE 227. PARRY *v.* WILKINSON.

1797, June 29.
PARRY, William, the elder, of Aldermanbury, London, merchant, complains that
WALKER, Emmanuel, late of Philadelphia, merchant, was partner with
LEE, John, who, in 1775, in Boston, New England, entered into partnership with
WILKINSON, Thomas, of Southwark, merchant, then in New York.
Action for an account.

In the Public Record Office, London.

CHANCERY PROCEEDINGS, 1758–1800.

BUNDLE 685. CRAMOND *v.* PERRY.

1799, Oct. 12.
CRAMOND, William,
LEAMY, John, and
HOLMES, Hugh, of Philadelphia, merchants, executors of
CAY, David, surviving partner of
CLOW, Andrew, deceased, trading in Pennsylvania.
Action for an account.

In the Principal Probate Registry, London.

P.C.C. 544 MARRIOTT.

1800, Nov. 29.
HARVEY, William, of Stoke Ferry, Norfolk, gent., his will names
HARVEY, John, my nephew, of New York.
Proved 21 June, 1803.

In the Records of the Drapers' Company, London.

1597, Nov. 21.
    ALKYN, Richard, made free by service with Thomas BARNEHAM, in Eastcheap, a band-seller, lynnen.
    [? 1598 June 29, married at Heston, Middx., Anna WHITHORNE. Will proved 1638, by relict Anne, " of St. Margaret Pattens," London. See June 1630, Sampson ALKYN.]

1603, March 21.
    WITTES, Thomas, apprenticed to BURTON, William. Made free 28 July, 1613. Of Coleman Street, silk weaver. Pays quarterage, 1617/23. *Later note:* " In Virginia."

1604, Jan. 9.
    LANGLEY, Richard, son of John, citizen and draper, apprenticed to brother John LANGLEY. Free by patrimony 22 Oct. 1613; married Alice LEISTER, 1617; pays quarterage, 1617/20; in 1626 (will of father) " beyond the seas." *Later note:* " In Virginia." Steward of Bethlem Hospital 1641.

1604, June 18.
    ASHBY, John, apprenticed to John STOCKS, seven years.
    [Made free of the company 7 July, 1613; takes apprentice Robert HIND, 28 Feb. 1615. Query, married 29 Jan. 1614, Siscellay SIVIER at St. Vedast, London. Note in Quarterage Book, 1628/40: " Virginia."]

1605, Nov. 6.
: CUNSTABLE, Thomas, made free by
WOLFE, Philip. In 1606 takes apprentice
BENNETT, William.
Later note: "A poor man at Virginia."

A.D.
1606. ASTLEY, Thomas, apprenticed to Robert THOMAS, 7 years.
: [Made free of the Company, 1613; pays quarterage, 1614–1617; takes apprentice Thomas ASHBY, or ASHLY, 1616; and George KEMIS, 1617. Notes in Quarterage Book, 1617/27: "gone to Virginia"; "in Virginia."]

1606, Feb. 18.
: JENNINGS, Thomas, made free by Robert JENNINGS. He was an upholster in Old Jewry, "decayed." Paid quarterage 1616–20. *Later note:* "In Virginia."

Duke of Northumberland's MSS.

(HIST. MSS. COMMISSION 3/53).

1607. June 22. James Town in Virginia. Letter. The Council in Virginia to the Council of Virginia in England. Refers to conditions of agriculture, &c.
NEWPORT, Captain [Christopher], and is signed by
WINGFIELD, Edward Maria,
SMITH, John,
MARTINE, John,
GOSNOLD, Bartholomew,
RATTCLIFFE, John, and
KENDALL, George. [Copy, 2 pp.]

In the Records of the Drapers' Company, London.

1609, Feb. 28.
    WHITNEY, Samuel, apprenticed to
    HUMBLE, Mark. Made free 16 April, 1619. A pointmaker.
    Later note: " In Virginia."

1616, Jan. 22.
    HAWLEY, Gabriel, son of James, of Brainford [Brentford], Middlesex, " generosus," apprenticed to
    PAVIER, William, for 9 years.
        Free of the company 6 July, 1636. On 11 July, 1636, takes apprentice
    BOROUGHES, John.
        Note in 1636/42 book : " in Virginia."
        [*See American Colonists*, First Series, page 23.]

1616, May 29.
    CANNON, Raphe, made free by
    HUMBLE, Mark, a pointmaker at the " Ship " tavern by the Exchange. In 1616, Nov. 13, a haberdasher of small wares in Birchin Lane. Pays quarterage, 1617/20. *Later note:* " Now in Virginia."

Acts of the Privy Council, England.

(*p.* 301.)

1617, July 13. Warrant for reprieve of
POTLEY, Christopher,
POWELL, Roger,
MOLINEUX, Sapcott, and
CHROUCHLEY, Thomas, prisoners in Oxford gaole, to be transported into Virginia, with proviso that they return not again into England.

(*p.* 61.)

1617/18. March 5. A letter to the Lord de la WARE.
Whereas Henry SHERLEY, son of Sir Thomas SHERLEY, Knight, imprisoned in the King's Bench for debt, hath made escape, and, as it is thought, will attempt to transport himself into Virginia, upon this occasion of your Lordship's going thither, we pray and require your Lordship not to suffer any such attempt. . . .

1617/18. March 20.
An open warrant to the High Sheriff of Middlesex for the reprieve of
LAMBE, William, prisoner in Newgate, to be imployed into Virginia.

In the Records of the Drapers' Company, London.

A.D.
1617/27. " In Virginia."
THOMSON, Nathaniel, apprentice 17 June 1607, to
CONSTABLE, Edward, 7 years. Made free 18 Jan. 1615.

Acts of the Privy Council, England.

(*p.* 285.)

1618, Oct. 31.
A warrant to reprieve Ann RUSSELL, prisoner in Newgate, to be delivered to Sir Thomas SMYTH, Knight, governor of the East India Company, to be employed by him into Virginia.

Nov. 30.
A warrant for the reprieve and embargement of James STRINGER, prisoner in Newgate, to be sent over and disposed of by Sir Thomas SMYTH, &c., into Virginia.

In the Principal Probate Registry, London.

P.C.C. 56 SOAME.

1619, Nov. 2.
LAWNE, Christopher, of Blanford, Dorset, " nowe lying in Charles Citie in Virginia " in his will names " my goods now in Virginia " ; wife Susanna ; sons Lovewell L. and Symon L., executors, both under 21.
OLLIFFE, Anne, my daughter in law, at marriage ; Robert O.
POWLE, Capt. Nathaniel,
MACOCKE, Mr Samuel, and
HAMOR, Capt. Ralph, to be overseers.
ANTHONY, Mr Lawrence, of the Poultrie in London.
ELLIS, Mr Richard, of St Sythinge's Lane in London.
WHITE, Mr John, of Ockford in Dorset, and
WILLIS, Mr William, of Woore in Dorset, overseers.
WEST, Nathaniel, and
FLYNTON, Pharao, are witnesses.
Admon. 17 June, 1620, to William WILLIS, during minority of Lovewell and Symon LAWNE.

In the Principal Probate Registry, London.

P.C.C. 8 SOAME.

1619, Dec. 2.

FERNE, John, of St Vedast, Foster Lane, London, yeoman, in his will gives " all my freehould landes and hereditaments in Virginia the Sommer Ilands and elswhere to my three sonnes John, James & Daniel FERNE. Lands in Harrow on the Hill, Middlesex. Son Daniel executor.

NEWARKE, Bridget, my daughter, wife of John.

LISNEY, Richard, to his two sons " a booke of all Mr GREENE-HAM'S workes."

BEEKE, John, and

MATHEWS, Edward, public scrivener, are witnesses.

Proved at London 7 Jan. 1619/20, by the executor named.

In the Principal Probate Registry, London.

P.C.C. 36 SOAME.

1619/20, March 11.

SHAWE, William, of Wapping, Middlesex, mariner " in this my present intended voyage to Virginia," in his will names his children John, Martha, Mary, Joane, Elizabeth and Sara (all under 21); brother Thomas S. of Haslington, Chester, yeoman; sister Anne, of Sandbiche, spinster; cousin John S., of London, goldsmith. Wife Martha executrix.

BROME, Margaret, my sister, wife of Hugh B., of Sandbiche, Chester, husbandman.

ABRAM, Cicely, my sister, of Haslington, widow.

CHAPMAN, Joseph, Jonathan & Samuel, my wife's brothers.

MEKIN, Robert, and

PAPWORTH, Robert, of London, chandler, executors.

GREENE, Richarde, scrivener, and

DEARSLYE, Jo., are witnesses.

Proved at London 11 Oct. 1620, by the executrix named.

In the Principal Probate Registry, London.

P.C.C. 32 SOAME.

1619/20, March 23.

FARRAR, Nicholas, citizen and skynner of London, of St Sythes Lane, St Benedict Sherhogg, in his will says "Whereas there is latelye given a begynnynge to the erectinge and foundinge of a Colledge in Virginea for the conversion of Infidells children unto Christian Religion . . . my executor shall give three hundred poundes unto the Company of Virginea . . . with the advice of

SANDYS, Sir Edwin, nowe Treasurer of the Company, and my sonn John FARRAR. To the poor of Harford where I was born £10. My house there called "The Bell." "To the worll. Companye of the Skynners whereof I am a brother three or fower Bowlles of Silver playne to drincke in of the valewe of Twenty marcks."

MIDDLETON, Sir Thomas, sometyme my partner, and Hugh M. WYCHE, Mr Richard, & others.

FARRAR, . . . , my daughter, & grandchild Nicholas F. My wife Mary F. Sons Nicholas (executor) and Richard.

COLLETT, John, my son and his wife, & Mary their daughter. My age is three score and fifteen.

SHEPHEARD, Thomas, Mary COLLETT and Richard FARRAR are witnesses.

Proved at London 4 April, 1620, by the executor named.

Acts of the Privy Council, England.

(*pp.* 206, 310, 356.)

1622, May 2.

A warrant for the reprieve of

FRANK, Daniel,

BEARE, William, and

IRELAND, John, now prisoners in The White Lion in Southwark, condemned for stealing cattle and for no other offence, to be delivered to the Governor of the Company of Virginia, to be conveyed to Virginia with speed.

1622, Aug. 12.
A similar warrant for
NORTON, James, convicted at Norwich for drawing of a purse, with order for sending him to Virginia.

1622, Nov. 20.
A similar warrant for
CARTER, John, convicted for stealing a horse; to transport him to Virginia.

From the Records of the Drapers' Company, London.

1623, March 26.
HAYNES, Richard, son of Francis, of Canterbury, needle-maker, apprenticed to
WILSON, Thomas, for 8 years, and made free by service 25 July, 1631. Pays quarterage in 1631. Notes: 1631/42 "in Lothbury," "in Virginia."

A.D.
1629/42. "Threadneedle street." "A poor fellow gone to Virginia."
CRAKE, Ralph, son of George, of Loftmarras, Yorks, generosus.
Apprenticed 1 July, 1619, to
LEAMING, Charles, a goldsmith in Noble street, for 9 years; made free 16 Dec. 1629.

1630, June.
ALKYN, Sampson, made free by patrimony, son of Richard, with his father in Eastcheap.
1631 and 1632 pays quarterage to the company. *Later note:* "In Virginia; goes thither and back."

In Rev. Dr. Williams' Library, London.

HIST. MSS. COMMISSION, 3RD REPORT, APP. 366.

A.D.
1630/70. An alphabetical list of ministers who settled in New England from 1630 to 1670, with the places at which they officiated; 4 ff.

In the Principal Probate Registry, London.

P.C.C. 145, 148 RIVERS.

1638, Aug. 4.
BULKELEY, Arthur, of London, marchant, bound for the Plantation of Virginia, in the good ship "The Blessing" of London, in his will names
SIMMORY, Mr William, master.
BULKELEY, Thomas, my brother, of the citty of London, marchant, sole executor.
KIGHTE, Hen., servant to
WARNER, John, scr., and
LEADBETTER, Samuel, witnesses.
   Proved at London 3 Nov., 1645, by Thomas BULKELEY, the brother.
   [148 RIVERS gives date of will as " 4 Aug. 1641."]

In the Records of the Drapers' Company, London.

1639, March 4.
INGLESBY, Mathew, son of William, of New England overseas, wheelwright, apprenticed to
SMITH, Edward. Made free 22 Sept. 1652; weaver, Mile End; several apprentices. Living 1668.

In the Principal Probate Registry, London.

P.C.C. 29 FAIRFAX.

1639, April 17.

ARCHER, John, clerk, who died abroad, his will names Fr. ARCHER, "my brother Theophilus," "my wife and child" under 21, "my brother Francis and my brother the scholar in New England," "All his Lattaine books to the scholar now at Rotterdam."

NYE, Philip, wrote this will and was witness.

Admon. 3 March, 1648/9, to Susan ARCHER, the relict.

In the Principal Probate Registry, London.

P.C.C. 112 FINES.

1640, Apl. 9.

STOLION, Jane, of London, widow, her will names her lands in Mayfield, Sussex, settled upon

HAYES, William, of Little Horsted, gent.,

MAYNARD, John, of Mayfield, clerke,

DURANT, Nicholas, of Headlith and

TURNOR, Thomas, of Caginer, yeoman.

"My daughter Elizabeth STOLION and my sons Abraham (executor) and Thomas STOLION."

EDWARDS, John, late of Cuckfield, gent., his son & heir in remainder.

"My personall estate in New England."

Proved 4 May 1647, by Abraham STOLYON, the son.

In the Principal Probate Registry, London.

P.C.C. 126 CAMBELL.

1642, Nov. 3.

HARWOOD, Arthur, " of the Island of Virginia in parts beyond the seas and now resiant in the parish of St Peter the advincle neere the Tower of London, marchant," in his will names Mrs Elizabeth H., Mr George H., George H., deceased, Leonard H., Sara and Barbara, daughters of John H., Ruth, dau. of Christopher H., Mrs Dorothie H., and her son Augustine.

RICHBELL, Mr William, and his three children; Andrew R., Edmond R.

SYMONDS, Mrs Sarah.

LAGEE, Mrs Susan.

PITCHFORKE, Helen, wife of Henry.

ANDERSON, Mr Richard.

LAURENCE, Arthur.

HARWOOD, Alexander, citizen and mercer of London, executor.

SMITH, Anne, and

YARWAY, Robert, scrivener, are witnesses.

Proved at London 12 Dec. 1642 by Alexander HARWOOD.

In the Principal Probate Registry, London.

P.C.C. 30 FINES.

1643, Aug. 13.

ALLEN, Thomas, of London, apprentice to

DENHAM, George, citizen and leatherseller, his will names

BIRCHAM, Elizabeth, my sister, now wife of Robert B.

BOZONNE . . . my brother, now in New England.

ALLEN, William, my brother, my houses called Coopers & Olds, &c., sole executor.

Proved 16 Feb. 1646/7, by the executor named.

In the Principal Probate Registry, London.

P.C.C. 221 NABBS.

A.D.
1643, Aug. 23.

MORTON, Thomas, of Cliffords Inn, London, gent., in his will names land in the province of Carlile, New England, 5000 acres on the East side of the River Quillepiocke and 5000 on the West side extending four miles along the river, in the province of Ligonia, 2000 acres in Casco Bay next the River Pesumskegg, the two Clupp Board Ilands in Casco Bay, Martin's Vyneyard Iland on the Southern side of Cape Codd nere Narohiganses Bay.

MILLES, Tobias, my cousin-german, and
BRUCE, Sara, widdowe, my neece, executors.
WOODWARD, William, servant to, and
FRYER, Thomas, witness.

Proved at London 9 August 1660 by Sara WILSON *alias* BRUCE one of the executors.

In the Principal Probate Registry, London.

P.C.C. 28 ESSEX.

1644, Dec. 14.

WILLYS, George, of Hartford upon Conecticot, his will names " my buildinges, landes, &c., in Hartford boundes and att Tuxus Seposs unto my beloved wife Mary, my sonnes Samuel and George . . . The west syde of the greate river in the boundes of Wetherfield unto my sonne George. My lands at Fenny Compton in Ould England . . . My daughter Hester £400. My daughter Amy £350 at marriage."

FENWICKE, M^r	HOOKER, M^r	
HAINES, M^r	STONE, M^r	
HOPKINS, M^r	WARRHAM, M^r	
WELLES, M^r	HUETT, M^{rs}	my friends.
WEBSTER, M^r	SMITH, M^r	
WHYTTING, M^r	GIBBINS, William	
MASON, Capt.		

HOPKINS, Edward, and GIBBINS, William, are witnesses.

Codicil 22 Feb. 1644/5. Edward HOPKINS, witness. Codicil 4 March, 1644/5, 40/s. to the poor of Winsore. Wits., Edward HOPKINS, William WHITINGE.

Admon. 9 Feb. 1647/8 to George WILLIS, the son, in the absence of Mary the relict.

In the Principal Probate Registry, London.

P.C.C. 87 RIVERS.

1645, April 26.

WHITEHEAD, Richard, "of Windsor, upon Conneckticott River in New England in the parts of America," in his will names "My messuage," &c., "The Crowne," in Knoll, Warwick, England, in occupation of

KNOLLES, Thomas, and

SHAKESPEARE, John

LEWES, Mary, my daughter in law £100 given her by my wife,

HOPKINS, Hugh, my brother in law, trustee,

WHITEHEAD, Mary, my wife, my brother Edward W.; his sons John and Edward; my brother Mathew W., and Joane his daughter.

ANDREWES, John, of Clifton, my brother and John his son,

FISHER, Joyce, my sister, her son & daughter Richard & Mary,

HIGGINS, Hannah, Sarah, Rebecca and Abigael, my kinswomen,

FISH, Mr Thomas, of Wedgneeke Pinke, my loving friend.

UNDERWOOD, Dorothie, his maydservant.

ROGERS, Edward.

EDWARDS, Mathew, and

SMITH, William, of Langley, to be overseers.

EEDE, Fran.

FISHE, Hester and Cr. and

PERKINS, Michael, are witnesses.

Proved at London 26 June 1645 by John ANDREWES.

In the Principal Probate Registry, London.

P.C.C. 115 ESSEX.

1645, Nov. 16.

BRADING, Nathaniel, "in Augustin Bay on the Isle of Madagascar," his will names "my honoured father Mr Wm BRADING of the Isle of Wight in the parish of Godsall" executor. Brothers James & Joseph & sister Ruth B. My mother Mrs Helen B.

KENT, Mr Richard, of Newberry, New England, my uncle.

SMART, Capt. John, governor of the plantation of Madagascar. Inventory of books, clothing, &c., annexed.

Proved at London 1 July 1648, by William BRADING.

In the Principal Probate Registry, London.

P.C.C. 31 FINES.

1645, Dec. 31.

MENEFIE, George, Esq., of Buckland in Virginia, in his will desires to be buried in the parish church of Westover. Names "the shipp 'Desire' now lying before Buckland." Tobacco to be consigned to

ANDREWS, Captain Peter.

My sixteenth part of the "William & George." To my daughter Elizabeth MENEFIE land at Westover, at James Citty and at Yorke River.

BISHOPP, John, my brother.

PERRY, Henry, my son in law.

JAMES, M^r Jo. to preach a sermon.

CONVERSE, M^r Jo., chirurgion, 2000 pounds of tobacco.

BOOKER, Roger, my brother.

LISTER, Humfrey, to collect debts.

1645, Dec. 31—*cont.*

WHITE, Jo., merchant, £50 to continue in Virginia one year. Tobacco to be laden upon " The Flower " of London, provided itt may goe for fower pounds sterlinge per tunn. Ship " Mary & George." My wife Mary to be executrix and guardian to my daughter Elizabeth.
VARVELL, Captain Tho., tobacco due to, to be satisfied by ASTON, Mr Walter.
ADLINGTON, Mr Humfrey, to be paid for his care in my business concerning CHAMBERLINE by my friend Capt. Peter ANDREWS. He and
BENNETT, Richard, Esq., overseers. Ship " Richard & Judith."
PRISE, Howell and Humfrey LISTER are witnesses.
Proved at London 25 Feb. 1646/7 by Mary MENEFIE the relict.

In the British Museum, London.

HARLEIAN MS. 1172.

A.D.
1646, OXWICK, Thomas, of London, living sometime in Virginia, his niece Jane, dau. of Robert O., of London, marchant, Captain of the Trained Band at Mitcham, Surrey.
ARMS, certified by William RYLEY, Lancaster Herald : *Argent, on a chevron engrailed azure betw. 3 bucks' heads erased sable attired or, as many cinquefoils of the last.* CREST—*From a mural coronet or, a bull's head sable, horned and crined of the first.*

In the Principal Probate Registry, London.

P.C.C. 73 FINES.

1646, Jan. 21.
PRYOR, William, his will, names Margaret, "my eldest daughter." My whole part of the ship "Honor." To my daughter Mary my land in Virginia. Proceeds of tobacco sent home this year.
CLAYTON, Jasper, my brother in law, his eldest son.
KEMPE, Richard, Esq., his wife.
BENNETT, Richard, Esq.
HARRISON, Thomas, captain of the ship "Honor."
KIRTON, Mrs. Mary, £100.
HARWOOD, Capt. Tho., overseer.
ROSE, John, and
HOCKADAY, William, are witnesses.
Admon. 15 April 1647, to CLAYTON & HARRISON during minority of the daughters. Admon. 12 Nov. 1660 to Mary PRYOR the daughter.

In the Principal Probate Registry, London.

P.C.C. 189 TWISSE.

1646, June 30.
WILLIAMSON, Richard, citizen & merchant taylor of London, his will names "my brother Roger WILLIAMSON, residing in Virginia," & his children. Cozens Thomas W., & Alice his sister, & Sarah W. Wife Mary executrix.
NIGHTINGALE, Anne, my cozen.
Proved 5 Dec. 1646 by the executrix. Administration 19 Nov. 1651 to Martha OLBOSTON, sister of the executrix, to the use of Sarah WILLIAMSON the brother's child of the testator.

In the Principal Probate Registry, London.

P.C.C. 148 TWISSE.

1646, Sept. 11.

ELBRIDGE, John, of St Peter's, Bristol, marchant, his will names his father's will dated 25 Feb. 1643, his vault or arched dormitorie in St Peter's church, divers lands in New England, brother Thomas, manor of Chellwood, Somerset. King James's letters patent 3 Nov., 18th year, to the President and Councell of New England. Their grant 29 Feb. 1631 " to my auncestors,"

ALDWORTH, Robert, and Giles ELBRIDGE of Bristowe, marchants, of one great continent of land 12000 acres, to make a plantacon. My uncle Robert A., alderman, of Bristol.

ELBRIDGE, Aldworth, my brother.

CUGLEY, Martha, widow, my sister. My neece Elizabeth CUGLEY.

MOORE, Elizabeth, my sister, now wife of Thomas M., marchant.

PAYNE, Elizabeth, my cozen, daughter of George P., of Bristol, marchant, and Elizabeth his wife.

CALE, Mr Nathaniell, of Bristol, soape boyler and my said brother Thomas ELBRIDGE, executors. Said brother now beyond the seas and in his minoritie. To said Mr CALE " my greate double gilt bowle."

Codicil 20 Sept. 1646. Proved 16 Oct. 1646 by Nathaniel CALE; power reserved for Thomas ELBRIDGE.

In the Principal Probate Registry, London.

P.C.C. 113 PEMBROKE.

1646, Sept. 15.
HARVEY, Sir John, of London, knight, in his will states that "whereas His Most Excellent Majestie King of England doth owe unto mee £5500," and also there are severall sumes of money due and owing unto mee from severall persons in Virginia, £2000. I owe unto
DIXON, Tobias, citizen & haberdasher, £1000, (executor), and unto NICKOLLS, M^r, of London, ironmonger, £200. I give unto Ursilla, my eldest daughter £1000, my daughter Anne £1000.
HARVEY, Symon, my nephew, eldest son of my late brother Sir Simon H., late of London, knight, £500, and £400 to the two daughters of the late Sir Simon.
Admon. 16 July 1650, to Alice, relict of Tobias DIXON, the testator having died beyond seas.

In the Principal Probate Registry, London.

P.C.C. 165 FINES.

1647, May 24.
TYLER, Grace, now wife of John TYLER of Colchester, Essex, say-weaver, her will, names
ALDOUS, James, late of Dennington, Suffolk, carpenter, my late husband. Richard A., of Winkfield, yeoman.
MONSER, Sauina, my sister, her children W^m & Henry M., and SMITH, Samuel, Richard and Sauina.
BROCK, Elizabeth, my sister, of Dedham in New England; John, Elizabeth & Anne her children.
BURGESSE, Sibilla, my late sister, her children John B., James, Peter, Sibilla & Elizabeth.
BROWNE, John, of Brundish, and
YOUNGES, William, of Cratfeild, my cosens, executors.
Proved at London 19 July 1647, by YOUNGES; power reserved for BROWNE.

In the Principal Probate Registry, London.

P.C.C. 186 PEMBROKE.

1647, Sept. 22.

PHIPPING, William, of Wedmore, Somerset, baker, in his will names "my daughters Frances and Elizabeth." "My brother Joseph PHIPPING in Ireland." Daughter Elizabeth executrix.

VAGE, Richard, overseer.
NUMAN, Richard.
ANDREWES, Ellinor, widow.
PEACOCKE, William, of Olom in the parish of Bitten, co. Gloucester.
BROWNE, Richard, overseer.
SMEASE, John, of Cocklock in the parish of Wedmore.
WEBB, Richard & Thomas, and
ADDAMS, William, are witnesses. To John ADDAMS my son in law, the house at Wedmore until the return of my daughter Judah out of New England.

Proved at London 9 Nov. 1650, by Elizabeth, wife of John ADDAMS, the executrix named.

In the Principal Probate Registry, London.

P.C.C. 325 BRENT.

1647, Nov. 3.

SMITH, Henry, of London, gent., in his will names John SMITH of St Paul's Alley, London, draper. The manor of Piratts *alias* Sawston, Cambs.

MUNDAY, Henry, now in New England (6 July 1652), & Edward (deceased), my nephews.
SANDALL, John, of Furnivall's Inne, Middlesex, gent.
HUDDLESTON, Henry, Esq.
SPURR, Katherine.
KENT, Valentine, my godson.
GILLAM, William, my old servant.
MOULT, Francis, my servant.
BERRIDGE, Richard, executor.
BLOUNT, Thomas, of London, gent., supervisor.

Proved at Westminster 3 May 1653 by the executor named.

In the Principal Probate Registry, London.

P.C.C. 122 GREY.

1648, May 18.

LATHAM, Andrew, of Bury, co. Lancaster, clarke, in his will makes Martha his wife executrix, and names his daughter, his brothers John and Paul L., sister Thomasine, Elizabeth & Susanna, sisters in law Anna, Elizabeth and Marie, and nephews Henry. & Paul, sons of John L.

BINS, Mr Thomas, of Halifax, my father in law.

He gives £5 " towards the advance of the Gospell amongst the poore Indians in New England " to be paid over to ASHURST, Mr Henry, of London, draper, who is to send the same to DUNSTAR, Mr Henry, President of the Colledge in Cambridge there.

RISLE, Thomas, & John, my nephews.

Proved at London 14 June 1650, by the executrix named.

In the Principal Probate Registry, London.

P.C.C. 126 ESSEX.

1648, July 14.

BURRELL, William, of Virginia, planter, in his will names " my brother " John B.

KARMIHILL, Anne, my sister, her two youngest daughters. (CARMICHAEL.)

KELLEY, Richard, my brother in law, executor.

WATSON, Richard, and

BROWNE, Richard, are witnesses.

Proved at London 4 August 1648 by the executor named.

In the Principal Probate Registry, London.

P.C.C. 122 FAIRFAX.

1648, Oct. 4.

HADDOCKE, William, " plainter, being now bound on a voyage to Virginia," in his will names " my last wives porcon," " my brother Richard HADDOCKE, girdler, bound for me by obligation to

CORY, John, stiller, for the payment of 46/s. sterling within ten days after the arrival of the shipp ' William and Anne ' from her now intended voyage to Virginia."

LUCKE, William, master of the said ship.
WHITBYE, William, at Virginia.
PURNELL, Arthur, of Virginia.
ADY, Ellen, spinster, a creditor.
HUGER, Thomas,
BURCHFILD, Matthew, and
WINDUS, James, scrivener, are witnesses.

Proved at London 27 August, 1649, by the executor named.

In the Principal Probate Registry, London.

P.C.C. 20 PEMBROKE.

1648, Nov. 30. Will of
ANDREWES, John, now resident in the Island of Barbadoes, names his brother Samuel A., executor, a minor.
SMITH, Mr Francis, clerk.
ELLIOTT, Mrs Mary, " my loving mother," wife of Henry E.
FENN, Deborah, my sister, wife of Robert FENN of Boston in New England, mariner.
SPRIGG, Thomas, and his wife Maudline.
POWELL, Morgan, and his wife Elizabeth.
MUNDAY, Edward,
BRETLAND, William,
ALLEINE, Bartue,
THORPE, James, and
DUDLEY, Arthur, are witnesses.
    Admon. 11 Feb. 1649/50 to Samuel WILD, guardian of Samuel ANDREWES, a minor, in the absence of POWELL and SPRIGG ; a former Admon. in March, 1648/9, to William CREEKE being revoked.

In the Principal Probate Registry, London.

P.C.C. 24 FAIRFAX.

A.D.
1649]. HOLMES, William, deceased abroad, in his will names his sons William and Robert, kinsman Mathye HOLMES' two children, "to the Master of the shipp if he will lett them goe to Vergenia £10." Olvere HOLMES, executor. The poore at Lugdin.
PARKINSON . . . my sister.
GRABE . . . my sister, and Richard G., my executor.
COXCE . . . my sister.
NICKLIS, M^r, ten shillings to make him a ring, and his wife 10/s.
PARKER, James, my brother, who dwells neare Canterbury.
JANSON, M^{rs}, my good countrey woman.
GRAYBEE, Richard, and
WALKER, Elizabeth, are witnesses. (No date.)
    Proved at London 16 Feb. 1648/9 by Oliver HOLMES and Richard GRABY, the nephews.

In the Principal Probate Registry, London.

P.C.C. 455 BERKELEY.

1649, Jan. 4.

KEMPE, Richard, of Kichneck, Virginia, Esquire, in his will desires "my body to be decently buried in my orchard." "My deare and carefull wife Elizabeth KEMPE and my poore child Elizabeth KEMPE my executryes." Mr Edward K., my brother; nephew Edmund K.

WORMELEY, Ralph, my unckle, executor during the minority of my child.

KEADO, Geo., to be granted fifty acres in the barren Necke where he liveth for my plantacon at Kappalianocke.

BENNETT, Master Richard, to make good the sale of my house at Towne.

LEE, Richard, my beloved friend.

BERKELEY, Sir William, to accept of £10. "I pray God to blesse this Colony."

RUHLEE, and

KEMPE, Edmund, witnesses.

Proved at London 6 Dec. 1656, by Elizabeth LUNSFORD *als.* KEMPE, the relict; Elizabeth, the daughter, and Ralph WORMLEY being dead.

In the Principal Probate Registry, London.

P.C.C. 132 PEMBROKE.

1649, April 2.

EWEN, William, of Greenwich, Kent, mariner, in his will names " Mary my wife," " my daughter Mary," " my ballast wharfe at Greenwich." Thomas EWENS the elder, and William and Thomas, Thomazine and Martha, his children.

JOHNSON, Ewen, and Margaret.

PETERS, Ewen, my kinsman (under 21), grandson of John EWEN.

PIGGOTT, Susan.

NOBLE, Mary, and her daughter, my cousins.

" All my lands, cattell, chattells and servants which I have in Virginia." My two shares of land in the Sommer Islands, 60 acres, in the occupation of

FARMER, William.

The North Mill standing upon the Deanes at Yarmouth.

STEVENS, William, my son in law, Thomas S., executor.

BROWNE, Arnold, executor.

Proved at London 12 Aug. 1650, by Mary EWENS, the relict.

In the Principal Probate Registry, London.

P.C.C. 92 FAIRFAX.

1649, April 30.

ELSEY, Nicholas, of Merstham, Surrey, yeoman, his will names "my sonne Nicholas which is as I hope in New England," "my sonne William." Nicholas, son of William ELSEY.

GANTON, Prudence, my sister.

SANDERS, Thomas, of Charlewood, who married the daughter of ANSCOMBE, William, of Merstham (overseer); Michael his son, executor.

BEEMAN, Thomas, my godson, a lame fellow.

BURSTONE, Alice, my servant.

BUCKNER, William, and

EATON, Nicholas, are witnesses.

Proved at London 22 June, 1649, by the executor named.

In the Principal Probate Registry, London.

P.C.C. 61 FAIRFAX.

1649, May 5.

PARKER, Judith, widow, of New England, in her will names Robert & Sarah, son & daughter of Thomas P., of Nedham Market.

SHEPHERD, Thomas, son of Thomas S. of Cambridge in Newe England.

WESTHORPE, Sarah, wife of Richard, one feather bedd, &c.

CARTER, widow.

MAY, widow.

WISEMAN, Elizabeth, widow.

MANNINGE, Robert, of Ipswich, executor.

DOUBBLE, John, senior and junior, halfe a crowne apeece.

VARONNE, Marie,

SOLOMON, Anne, and

CHAPMAN, James, are witnesses.

Proved at London 24 May 1649, by the executor named.

In the Principal Probate Registry, London.

P.C.C. 127 FAIRFAX.

1649, July 15.

TICE, William, who died abroad unmarried, in his will names " my eldest sister Mary TICE ; sister Anne TICE living in New England." " My brother in law two sonnes Walter TICE the eldest, Peeter TICE the youngest." " My friends at Umbra." " Persons legacies residing in India."

KINGE, Thomas, his children, and a girl born since named

HORDER, Susan, & William (executor).

DRANT, M^r, minister, and poor of Motcombe, Dorset, " where I was borne."

DUN, Joane.

ALDER, Mr John, and

NOKE, Mr William, to be overseers.

GOODYERE, John.

WILSON, John.

HILL, Harmen.

ROYDEN, Mr Verity.

OXENDEN, Mr George, my case of barber's instruments tipt with silver.

ANTHONY, Mr John, chirurgion.

WALLIS, Francis.

MOJAR, William, my cosen.

STEVENS, George, a taylor in Bell Yarde nigh Temple Barre, [London], his children.

LEWIS, John.

BENNETT, Thomas.

BAZY, Robert.

COLLY, Thomas, carpenter.

NAYLOR, John.

CROUCH, John, my cozen.

SMITH, Robert, executor.

YOUNG, H., and

GOLIPHER, Walter, are witnesses.

MORETAN, Jane, dwelling in Kenton, Devon, £3.

Proved at London 24 Aug. 1649, by Robert SMITH ; power reserved for the other executors named.

In the Principal Probate Registry, London.

P.C.C. 54 PEMBROKE.

1649, Oct. 10.

PARKER, Dorothy, of Mildenhall, Wilts, widow, in her will names her son Mr Thomas PARKER in New England, and gives him £200 now in the hands of

STEVENS, Mr Richard, my brother, of Stanton Bernard, Wilts.

AVERY, Elizabeth, my daughter, wife of Mr Timothie A., and her children.

BAYLY, Mr Thomas, my son.

WOODBRIDGE, John and Benjamin.

KERRIDGE, Sarah, and

SPARHAWKE, Lucy, the four children of my daughter Sarah BAYLY, executrix, with her son Mr Benjamin WOODBRIDGE.

TAYLOR, Mr John, my cozen, overseer.

Proved 20 April, 1650, by Benjamin WOODBRIDGE.

In the Principal Probate Registry, London.

P.C.C. 139 PEMBROKE.

1649, Nov. 30.

WALTON, Walter, son of Joan WALTON, living in England at Spofforth, Yorks, in his will refers to "this my voyage in the Hopeful Adventure now in Verginney bound for Maryland."
EWES, Mr Alexander, and
LAWSON, Mr Richard, my executors.
UNDERHILL, John, and
COWELL, Benjamin, of the said ship.
DAGORD, Henry.
SMITH, John, a passenger.
AISBE, Simson.
FOORD, Nathaniel.
WALKER, Peter.
MAY, Thomas, Peter WALKER, John ADDAMS, Miles COOKE, and Richard STEDMAN are witnesses.
Proved at London 17 Aug. 1650, by Richard LAWSON; power reserved for Alexander EWES.

In the Principal Probate Registry, London.

P.C.C. 61 PEMBROKE.

A.D. 1650].

BULLOCKE, William, "of Essex, gent., now bound for Virginia" in his will names "my wife, (of whose fidelitie and wisdome I have had good experience), my daughter Frances and my sonne Robert." "I make my said wife Mrs Elizabeth BULLOCKE my full and whole executrix."
HARRISSON, Tho., and
MILLS, Richard, are witnesses. (No date.)
Proved at London 10 May, 1650, by the executrix named.

In the Principal Probate Registry, London.

P.C.C. 391 ALCHIN.

1650, Jan. 8.

PORTMAN, Robert, bound for Ireland, in his will names his sister Margaret P., executrix.

MONTAGUE, Peter, the son of Peter M., in Virginia ; Margaret M., daughter of the said Peter.

DERE, Elizabeth, Anne & Mary, daughter of Pierce D.

GRINHILL, Captain John, overseer.

DEARE, Pierce & Edward, and

WILLIAM, John, are witnesses.

Proved at Westminster 22 Aug. 1654, by the executrix named.

In the Principal Probate Registry, London.

P.C.C. 173 GREY.

1650, Jan. 11.

HARRIS, Priscilla, of Northam, Devon, spinster, in her will names " my sister Agnes living in New England and her children." Cozen Rebecca H. My brother Richard HARRIS executor.

GRIBLE, Mary, my sister.

BAKER, Priscilla, my cozen.

STRABRIDGE, Bartholomew, my cozen.

HARRIS, Richard, my brother, his daughters.

GREAD, Phillip, my sister ; John, my brother-in-law.

LEIGH, William, my master & mistress, and

BARRY, Mr John, their son in law ; Mr William & his sister Honor.

SHAPTON, Bartholomew, the younger, his two sisters & brother John.

DAVIES, Anthony, his daughter Priscilla.

BARRY, John, and Richard BARTLETT are witnesses.

Proved at London 12 Sept. 1651 by the executor named.

In the Principal Probate Registry, London.

P.C.C. 53 GREY

1650, Feb. 19.
> SMITH, Nathaniel, in his will speaks of " money and goods that are now in New England " ; " my uncle John SMITH."
>
> CORWIN, Mr George.
>
> EDWARDS, Thomas, my kinsman, and Nathanael E., my cousin, executors.
>
> HALFORD, Ruth, my sister.
>
> NICOLLS, Mr John, flaxsman.
>
> BROWN, James.
>
> MAKEPEACE, Master.
>
> MELLOWES, Hanna, my sister, in New England.
>
> WANDLEY, Mr Samuel, my brother. My sister WANDLEY.
>
> FISHER, Mr Samuel, my brother.
>
> WALFORD . . . , my sister.
>
> BRIMSMEADES, Sam, and
>
> OLIVER, Samuel, are witnesses.
>
> Admon. 20 March 1650, to Thomas & Nathaniel EDWARDS.

In the Principal Probate Registry, London.

P.C.C. 95 NABBS.

1650, Feb. 25.
> HYDE, Sir Henry, knt., " in the Tower " [of London], in his will desires to be buried " in the Cathedrall Church of Salisbury neere my deceased parents . . . with an inscription that I suffered temporall death for loyalty." He names his brothers Dr Thomas, Dr James HYDE, Dr Edward HYDE. " My lands, &c., in the Somer Islands and Verginia to my godson William HYDE."
>
> VIVIAN, Mrs Frances.
>
> CROW, Henry, my godson.
>
> GOUNTER . . . , my sister and her husband, &c.
>
> Codicil, 1 March, 1650.
>
> Proved at London 23 June, 1660, by Dr Thomas HYDE and Dr James HYDE, the brothers.

In the Principal Probate Registry, London.

P.C.C. 63 GREY.

1650, May 8.

CHANDLER, Edward, of Ware, co. Hertford, draper, in his will names his wife Elizabeth, son Edward, son Jobe, son Noah, son Daniel, daughter Susan, houses in Ware & Hertford, purchased of
BEECKE, Will, and
BRETT, John, of London, linen drapers, and
GEATES, John, of Hunsdon, bricklayer.
HOLLY, Mary, my daughter.
CHANDLER, Daniel, my son, £10 " to be sent him over in comodities to Verginea." My daughter Sara CHANDLER now in Verginea. My youngest daughter Rebecca, under 18, and my daughter Martha under 21. Wife Elizabeth and son Edward executors.
LOVE, William, and
RANDALL, Mary, are witnesses.
Proved at London 24 April, 1651, by the executors named.

In the Principal Probate Registry, London.

P.C.C. 144 GREY.

1650, May 8.

HOOKER, Col. Edward, citizen and tallow chandler of London, of St Mary at Hill, in his will names his late wife Mrs Ellen HOOKER, buried in Mary Hill church. Gives to the repair of Chalcombe church and chancel 20 marks. Fifty eight poor men "to accompany my corps." My brother Peter, Ralph and Henry HOOKER his sons & Sibbell his daughter, Anne HOOKER, eldest daughter of my late brother Richard, and Mary HOOKER her sister that is now in New England. My cousin Edward HOOKER of Chalcombe & John his brother. My son Cornelius.

BOYSE . . . , my brother & sister, godson Edward; John, son of Henry BOYSE, deceased.

EGER . . . , my sister, Edward & Rose EGER, Jane my sister EGER's daughter.

WOODES, John, my cousin & his wife.

UNDERHILL, M^{rs}, at Brumley in Kent, my wife's sister.

ALMOND . . . , her sister.

Wife Elizabeth & son Cornelius executors.

Proved at London 16 July, 1651, by Cornelius HOOKER, Elizabeth, the relict, having renounced.

In the Principal Probate Registry, London.

P.C.C. 90 PEMBROKE.

1650, May 21.

DARBY, Agnes, relict of Augustine DARBY, of Bisley, Surrey, in her will nuncupative named Henry DARBY in New England £10, Richard DARBY 5/s, John DARBY twelve pence, Austen DARBY, my youngest son.
COLLIER, Henry, of Horsell, yeoman, executor.
LEE, Margaret, wife of John.
ELLIS, John, my son.
BOWBRICK, Joane, wife of Thomas.
BLONDALL, Thomas,
HOPKINS, Christopher, and
LEE, Henry, are witnesses.
Proved at London 18 June, 1650, by the executor named.

In the Principal Probate Registry, London.

P.C.C. 57 BOWYER.

1650, July 20.

FITZPEN *alias* PHIPPEN, George, clerk, in his will refers to his adherence to the Parliament and an Oxford decree pretended against him by
CATCHER, John.
His land in Enodes, Cornwall. To my brother David PHIPPEN in New England his eldest son the lesser Trewoone, to his second and third sons Trevosa. Mary my wife executrix, " her vertuous and respectfull deportment towards me."
PENROS, John, my brother.
Poor of Weymouth in Dorset & Melcombe.
Proved at London 1 March 1651/2 by relict Mary.

In the Principal Probate Registry, London.

P.C.C. 77 GREY.

1650, Aug. 1.

ARTHINGTON, Robert, of London, grocer, "being about to take a voyage to Virginia," in his will names "my brothers Mr Thomas ARTHINGTON & Mr John ARTHINGTON."
HODGES, Jane, my niece, under 18, to marry with consent of ELDRED, Mris. Marie, her aunt, my deare sister, executrix.
ROBERTS, Mistris Elizabeth, my cousen.
CLIPSHAM, Michael, and
WEEDEN, Lazarus, are witnesses.
Proved at London 13 May 1651 by the executrix named.

In the Principal Probate Registry, London.

P.C.C. 164 GREY.

1650, August 8.

REELEY, William, of Poplar in Stepney, Middlesex, in his will names "moveables belonging to me upon the James Island."
DUKE, Robert.
BAULDINE, Thomas.
DIMONDS, Ralph.
HIPKIS, John.
PEART, William.
BUBBE, John, and
SHEAPHARD, George.
NEWLAND, William,
GOODALL, Edward, and
EADES, John, are witnesses.
Admon. 22 Aug. 1651 to George SHEPPARD the "principall legator." The testator died "in the parts beyond the seas."

In the Principal Probate Registry, London.

P.C.C. 98 GREY.

1650, Sept. 16.

SEWARD, John, of Bristol, merchant, (being bound to sea on a voyage intended), in his will names "my daughters Sarah, Mary & Rebecca" under 21. John SEWARD my eldest son, under 21; son James. My farm in Butcombe, Somerset, purchased of Thomas PARSYVALL, Esq.

EYTON, Bridget, my wife's daughter by her former husband. My plantation, 1350 acres, inhabited, called Levinecke scituate in the Ile of Wight County in Virginia, to my son John SEWARD. My plantation and landes at Blackwater in the said county, 1600 acres. My wife Sarah, executrix.

CAREY, William, of London, merchant.
YEOMANS, Francis, of Bristow, gent., and
STEPHENS, Walter, the younger, of Bristoll, mercer, overseers.

Proved at London 23 May 1651, by Sarah, the relict.

In the Principal Probate Registry, London.

P.C.C. 26 GREY.

1650, Oct. 1.

KELWAY, Walter, of Chelmsford, Essex, in his will names "my wife Joanna" executrix. "My land in Writtle called Cheanes." "My grandchild Eliz. KELWAY, daughter of my son Jonathan, deceased.

MOUNTAGUE, Margaret.
SNOW, Melcas, and
LANE, Mary, my three daughters, all in New England.
ROPER, John, my grandchild.
CAUNTE, Ruth, my daughter.

My daughter Marie LANE at Boston in New England.
HOLBROUGH, Mr Richard, to be my overseer. He and
KELLUM, Sarah, are witnesses.

Proved at London 28 Feb. 1650/51, by Joanna K., the relict.

In the Principal Probate Registry, London.

P.C.C. 39 GREY.

1650, Nov. 14.

SMITH, John, gentleman, of Southwold, Suffolk, in his will names "my eldest son John SMITH." The house called the Lyon in Southwold. Son Robert. Daughters Anne, Mary & Phebe. Unto my wife a house and all debts and estate in New England. My sister Phebe SMITH. My wife Hellen SMITH executrix.

SPURDANCE, Mr Thomas, my son in law, and Mr William SMITH my cozen to be supervisors.

CUTLORD, Bartholomew,

WARREN, Ellen, and

MANINGE, Elizabeth, are witnesses, with John SMITH and Anne SMITH.

Proved at London 8 Feb. 1650/51 by Ellen SMITH, the relict.

In the Principal Probate Registry, London.

P.C.C. 135 GREY.

A.D.
1651.] WILSON, Robert, the son of Richard WILSON, chirurgeon, deceased, in his will names brother John WILSON. The Chamber of London.

JACOB, Andrew, "my father," & Katherine "my mother."

WALKER, Henry, "my friend," and

SMITH, George, are witnesses. (No date.)

Admon. 1 June 1651 to Katherine JACOB, the mother of the testator, "late beyond the seas in the parts of Virginia, a bachelor, deceased."

In the Principal Probate Registry, London.

P.C.C. 88 GREY.

1651, April 5.
HALSTED, Abraham, of Rotterdam, marchant, in his will names Darkes (Dorcas) HALSTED my wife, (executrix). My two sons Abraham and Isaac. My sister in New England.
SCHAPES, Will, my brother, marchant, executor.
WHITEMAN, Rebecka, my wives sister; James W., her brother.
BRAEN, Crist, my servant.
COCHROFT, Will, deceased, his three children.
LISTER . . . , my servant.
ARMYE . . . , my brother, his children.
COCKE . . . , my brother, his children.
KINGE, Mrs Rebecca, my former wives mother.
DAVIES, M^r, my father in lawe his children, and Gemeliell his children. "Expressly excepting against the manner of this country in the way of the Weasehouse."
Proved at London 2 May 1651 by Dorcas WHITMAN *alias* HALSTED, one of the executors.

In the Principal Probate Registry, London.

P.C.C. 196 GREY.

1651, June 26.
RAYMENT, George, of St John's in Glaston, Somerset, his will names "my son Maurice R., his wife & child," William RAYMENT my son & Elizabeth R., my daughter, that is in New England. John RAYMENT my son that is in New England.
ROBINS, Dorothy, my daughter and her children. Her husband of Streete.
SEEMER, William, his son John and daughter Luce, of Glaston. My son Maurice executor. William SEEMER and
BILLOCKES, William, overseers.
ZEALEE, William, and
ROSIER, George, are witnesses.
Proved 30 Oct. 1651, by the executor named.

In the Principal Probate Registry, London.

P.C.C. 73 BOWYER.

1651, June 27.

GROOME, Nicholas, in his will names his brother Henry GROOME and his children Marie, Elizabeth and Rence; his brother Mathew GROOME and his two children; his brother John GROOME and his son John; his sister Margett and her two daughters. "My plott, quadrant and compasses."

WALL, . . . , my brother & sister. Thomas WALL uplander in the Barbadoes, deceased.

GOOSE, . . . , my brother and John.

THORNEBUSH, . . . , my Aunt.

Arrival of the ship Castle in the River of Theames.

NURRY, Nicholas, the elder, and his son Nicholas late deceased.

ELICOTT, M^r, debts in his hands, and in those of

GUD, Captain, and

SPILLARD, M^r.

FORD, Thomas and Robert MECHELL are witnesses.

Proved at London 10 April 1652, by—WALL & Henry GROOME, the testator having died in Virginia.

In the Principal Probate Registry, London.

P.C.C. 242 BRENT.

1651, August—.

WILLIAMS, Richard, late of the parish of Catherine Creechurch, London, batchelor, deceased, "being bound for a voyage to Virginea in the service of this Commonwealth of England in the shipp called the John" did declare his will. To

HAWKINS, Walter, of the said parish, also bound for the said voyage but did go in another shipp, all my personal estate whatsoever, executor.

FARRAR, JOHN, and

FRENCH, Jane, are witnesses.

Proved at Westminster 11 May 1653 by the executor named.

In the Principal Probate Registry, London.

P.C.C. 149 BOWYER.

1651, Sept. 24.

IRBY, Walter, of Akeemacke, Northampton, Virginia, planter, in his will gives his mother Olive IRBYE *alias* COOPER, widow, his land, &c., in Hoggstrapp, county of Lincoln, makes her executrix, and names his late Aunt Anne IRBY, deceased.
DOBBETT, Ann, widow, in occupation of said land, &c.
MAY, Rebecka, and
WELSON, Thomas, scrivener, are witnesses.
Proved at London 30 July 1652, by Olive IRBY, the mother.

In the Principal Probate Registry, London.

P.C.C. 367 BRENT.

1651, Oct. 6.

INGRAM, Joseph, " being now bound for Virgine," in his will names " my father and mother ; " brothers Thomas, Robert, John and William ; sister Hester. " My native town of St. Ives." My father Robert INGRAM executor.
SMITH, Anne, my sister ; Anne SMITH her daughter, under 18.
INGRAM, Robert, jun^r, John INGRAM, and
BLYHTON, John, are witnesses.
Proved at Westminster 22 Sept. 1653 by the executor named.

In the Principal Probate Registry, London.

P.C.C. 202 BOWYER.

1651, Oct. 6.

STAGG (STEGGE), Capt. Thomas, " now bound forth to Sea in a voyage to Vergenia," in his will names his sister Alice ; brother Christopher's two daughters. The good ship " The Seaven Sisters." To my son Thomas STEGG in Vergenia my whole estate in Vergenia. The ship " Increase." My wife Elizabeth STEGG executrix.

1651, Oct. 6—*cont.*
> READE, Emelion, my wives sister.
> BYRD, Grace, my daughter, and her children; Elizabeth her daughter.
> BEALE, M^r, his houses in Bedlam I bought.
> LOTON, M^r, ...
> DRAITON, Mr Roger, and
> EARLE, Mr Robert, to be overseers. (No witnesses.)
> Proved at London 24 July 1652 by the executrix named.

In the Principal Probate Registry, London.

P.C.C. 228 BOWYER.

1651, Nov. 10.
> NICKOLSON, Robert, of London, merchant, and son of Francis NICKOLSON, Esquire, in Ipswich, in his will gives £10 towards the release of the English captives in Turkey. He is to be buried at the Barbadoes or in Virginia. He names " my brothers and sisters," my eldest brother Mr Francis N.
> PICKETT, M^r, minister of Chappell *alias* Pontibridge in Essex.
> MATTHEWES, Capt. Sam., of Virginea, Esquire, his wife, his son Sam. and his brother.
> BERNARD, Mrs Mary, of Warwicke River, widow, and her daughter.
> WOODERIFE, Stephen, gloves and ware which he oweth me.
> YOUNGE, John, master of the ship " Peter " of London, and his wife.
> RICHARDS, Mr John.⎫
> FAWNE, Mr Thomas ⎬ witnesses.
> STONE, John. ⎭
> DRIVER, M^r
> FREISBY, M^r
> JOHNSON, . . . , mate.
> MURRELL, M^r
> CORBIN, John.
> BEHEATHLAND, M^{rs} daughter to
> VERNALD, Mrs Mary, of Warwicke River, widow.
> Admon. 26 August 1652 to Francis NICKOLSON the father.

In the Principal Probate Registry, London.

P.C.C. 220 BOWYER.

1651, Dec. 25.
FAWNE, Thomas, who died abroad, in his will names the poor of Skendley (Skendleby) parish in Lincolnshire. My father and mother ; my brother Robert.
WILLIAMS, Robert, chirurgion of the ship called " The Peter."
MARTIN, William, my servant, I give him his passage to Virginia & his freedom there.
HATCH, M^r, woollen draper.
CRAYFORD, M^r
DAGGER, Thomas.
MURRELL, M^r
RICHARDS, Mr John.
PRESSON, D^r
CORBIN, M^r
JOHNSON, Matt.
YOUNGE, John and John STONE executors in Virginia.
FRISBY, James, witness.
Proved at London 17 Aug. 1652 by John YOUNG.

From the Records of the Drapers' Company, London.

A.D.
c. 1651. " Gone to Virginia."
GREGORY, William, free by redemption 8 Jan. 1650, takes as apprentice
JUBBS, Ralph.
Salesman in Birchin Lane [probably son of Henry GREGORY of Hunton, Kent, yeoman, dead in 1645, and apprenticed to COOKE, John, citizen and draper 3 Dec. 1645.]

In the Principal Probate Registry, London.

P.C.C. 320 BRENT.

1652, Jan. 28.

TORKINGTON, Joseph, of Virginia, planter, in his will names his brother Samuel TORKINTON, citizen and grocer of London his sole executor and universal legatee.
CROPTON, Zach.
HOTHERSALL, John.
HOPKINS, Richard.
AKEHURST, Harbert, and
BRIDGMAN, Edward, are witnesses.
Proved at Westminster 26 April, 1653, by the executor named.

In the Principal Probate Registry, London.

P.C.C. 278 BRENT.

1652, July 19.

GILES, Mascal, of Wartling, Sussex, clerke, in his will names his wife Frances. "My sonne Edward to be transported into New England, Virginia, or the Barbadoes, there to serve a Master for a terme of yeares." My daughter Mercy under 21. My son Samuel executor.
BROWNE, Benjamin, Martha and Peter (deceased), my wives children.
AUGUR, . . . , my sister.
CLERKE, Mr Edward, of Gutter Lane, London, grocer.
HOBEME . . . , my daughter.
FRERE, Mr Robert, of Plumton, my cozin,
BARTIN, Mr John, of Wartling,
CLERKE, Mr George, of Herstmonceux,
COBY, Mr Henry, of Hailsham,
HART, Mr David, of Wartling, and
BURDET, Mr Richard, to be overseers.
Proved at Westminster 27 April, 1653, by Samuel GILES.

In the Principal Probate Registry, London.

P.C.C. 237 BOWYER.

1652, Aug. 22.

ROCHE, James, of Warras Sweeke *alias* Warwicke Sweeke or the Isle of Wight in Virginia, planter, but now of Queene Camell *alias* Eat Camell, Somerset, his will recites that "whereas I sett sayle out of Virginia for England," 1st Jan. 1649, "and left behind mee a stocke of cattell . . . in the hands and care of

NORTH, Thomas, my servant."

FADDING *alias* FAWDIN, Capt. George, of Warras Quicke.

TABERER, Thomas, planter there.

My eldest brother ROCHES, vicar of Queene Camell, executor.

Proved at London 18 Sept. 1652, by Robert ROCHE, the brother.

In the Principal Probate Registry, London.

P.C.C. 165 BOWYER.

1652, Sept. 3.

WATSON, William, citizen and blacksmith of London, in his will names his wife Dorothie, the children of his brother Richard WATSON by his first and second wives, brother John & his son, brother Thomas's two daughters, brother Joseph & his two children, brother James WATSON, daughter Rebecca now resident in New England & her children.

FRANCKE, Magdalen, my sister, and her children.

HUBBARD, John, & Richard, my cousins.

Son Theodore WATSON a minor, daughters Hester & Ruth.

PALLMER, Edward, and

ROLLINSON, Thomas, of London, coopers, my cozens, executors.

HOARE, Daniel, and

BUTLER, John, scrivener, are witnesses.

Proved at London 4 Oct. 1652 by the executors named.

In the Public Record Office, London.

CHANCERY DEPOSITIONS, ELIZ.–CHAS. I.

BOND *v.* MOTTLE.

1652, Sept. 14.

FRY, Philippa, deceased, held copyhold in the manor of Combe St Nicholas, Somerset, now held by her daughter CLARKE, Ann, for lives of said Ann & George Fry.

[Probably widow of George FRY, sen^r, of Combe St Nicholas, taxed there in 1620, and died before 1629, and these in all probability the parents of George FRY of Combe St Nicholas, who died at Weymouth, Mass., in 1676.—*Somerset and Dorset Notes and Queries* 18/262.]

In the Principal Probate Registry, London.

P.C.C. 230 BRENT.

1652, Oct. —.

HARRISON, Nicholas, late of Virginia, planter, but dying in the parish of St Sepulchre's, London, by his will nuncupative or by word of mouth did give unto his mother Dorothy HARRISON all his estate whatsoever.

Admon. 28 Sept. 1653 to Dorothy HARRISON, the mother.

From the Records of the Drapers' Company, London.

A.D.

c. 1652. "Gone to New England."

DAVIS, Humphrey, (or DAVYE) son of John, of Sandford, Devon, Esquire, apprenticed 8 Dec. 1641, to

CHAUNDLER, George, merchant adventurer, Angl. member, East Indies Co., for 8 years. Made free of the company, 1652, lived in Bartholomew Lane. Merchant adventurer and member of East Indies Co.

[Qy. Humphrey DAVIS, who married Alice HARTRAM at Stepney, 1652 ?]

In the Principal Probate Registry, London.

P.C.C. 327 ALCHIN.

1653, Jan. —.
WALTER, Richard, in his will gives to his wife Sarah WALTER " all my debts and goods I have in the world."
Admon. 25 Feb. 1653/4 to Sarah, the relict; the testator "late of Newe England in the partes beyond the seaz." Admon. 5 Feb. 1661 to Thomas LUCKE the husband and administrator of the goods, &c., of Sara LUCKE *alias* WALTER, deceased, relict.

In the Principal Probate Registry, London.

P.C.C. 163 BERKELEY.

1653, March 14.
WOTTON, William, of Bristol, his will, in the form of a letter to his sister, dated "Virginie," names "my brother Arthur."
GOUGH, Mr Giles.
WINTOWER, . . . , my Aunt.
WINTER, Mrs Phillipp.
BARBER, Susanna, my sister.
GAWARD, . . . , my sister, and Mr GAWARD, her husband.
PHILLIPP, . . . , my sister.
SHARPHAM, . . . , my sister.
MEREDITH, Mary, my sister.
PALE, M^r.
GRIG, Captain.
PAULE, M^r & M^{rs} " as yet I cannot here of her brother for the want of his Master's name."
" Direct your letter to Mr FREER's house livinge in Chickahomine river neare James Cittie in Virginie."
Codicil, 13 Oct. 1653.
STEEVANS, John, and
JENINGS, Richard, are witnesses.
Proved at London 12 May, 1656, by Mary MEREDITH, the sister.

In the Principal Probate Registry, London.

P.C.C. 332 BRENT.

1653, April 17.

DOWNE, Nicholas, of London, Esquire, in his will wishes to be buried in the parish church of St Margrett's, Westminster, names his wife Ann executrix, and gives her all his estate in England, Virginia, or elsewhere. "To my neece Joane DOWNE if shee be living in Virginia one thousand pound weight of Tabacco, . . . Lieut. Coll. Bridges FREEMAN to deliver it to her in Virginia."

MULLARD, Joshua,
BARMBY, Bryan, and
JOHNSON, Jo., are witnesses.

Proved at Westminster 21 May, 1653, by the executrix named.

In the Principal Probate Registry, London.

P.C.C. 252 ALCHIN.

1654, May 13.

WHITTACRE, George, passenger aboard the good shipp called the William of London, bound from Virginia to London, his will names

DUCKWORTH, Edward, of St Clement Danes, London.
SCOTT, William, executor.
WEBBER, M^r, his shipp had aboard six pounds of sugar.
WILLIAMS, Solomon, and
JAMES, Owen, witnesses, sworn before
PASKE, William, 26 June, 1654.

Proved at Westminster 26 June, 1654, by William SCOTT.

In the Principal Probate Registry, London.

P.C.C. 391 ALCHIN.

1653, July 29.

PERCEY, Richard, now belonging to the "Two Brothers" in the parts of Virginia, his will names his wife Annis PERCY executrix.
EVANS, George.
FOULLARD, Thomas, seaman.
GARNSEY, John.
INGRAM, Giles.
HARRIES, Abraham.
EASTWOOD, Abraham.
FULLER, Thomas, and
SPARKE, George, are witnesses.
Proved at London 31 March, 1654, by the executrix.

In the Principal Probate Registry, London.

P.C.C. 389 ALCHIN.

1653, Nov. 2.

CONVERS, John, in his will names his wife Susanna, executrix; son John; brother Will. CONVERS his children; daughter Lucy C., by late wife Lucy, to whom money due on death of her grandmother and of her brother Thomas, now living, in the hands of
BUSHELL, Mr Edward, marchant.
Fox, Captain John, overseer, in Verginia. My cargo in the ship "Thomas & Anne," £379 15s. 4d. Mrs Elizabeth Fox.
LOWFIELD, Mr Will.
CUTLING, Mr John.
LEE, Mr Henry, of Yorke river.
JORDAINE, Mary, my sister, and her children.
PHILLIPS, Anthony, my cozen garman.
RAWLINGS, Geromiah, servant.
Proved at Westminster 1 May, 1654, by the executrix named.

In the Principal Probate Registry, London.

P.C.C. 233 BERKELEY.

1654, Feb. 10.

PIERCE, Mark, of London, in his will names " Samuel, Mark, Debora & Sarah, children of my brother Henry PIERCE."
NEWMAN, Robert, citizen and vintner of London, executor.
SWANN, Master William, at the house of
LUDLOWE, Master, in Dublin.
CAFFINCH, Master Samuel.
HIGGINSON, Elizabeth, widow of Theophilus H., in New England.
DEVENPORT, Master, pastor at Newhaven in New England.
VINER, Master William, citizen and joyner, executor.
DONE, Rebeka & Anne, daughters of my brother in law Fromabove DONE.
BROOKE, Samuel, Elizabeth, & Dorothy, children of my sister Sarah B., deceased.
EDGER, Libia, daughter of
ELLIS, Jane, my sister, deceased.
MARSHALL, Jerome, and
GILBERTE, Nicholas, are witnesses. Long inventory of goods.
Proved at London 3 June, 1656, by VYNER and NEWMAN.

In the Principal Probate Registry, London.

P.C.C. 231 AYLETT.

1654, April 4.

WILSON, Thomas, in the countie of Middlesex, mariner, and commander of the ship " Charles " now in Virginia, his will names his " wife Ellinor and all my children." She executrix.
LUDLOWE, Col. George.
CANT, Master David, my loving countryman.
MARTIN, Nicholas, and
PRISE, John, are witnesses.
Proved at London 17 Jan. 1654–5, by the executrix named.

In the Principal Probate Registry, London.

P.C.C. 313 AYLETT.

1654, Sept. 9.

LATHBURY, John, citizen and pewterer of London, intending to take a voyage to sea, in his will names " my brother Thomas LATHBURY."

KIRKHAM, Robert, my brother, and Richard K.

DRURY, John, citizen & pewterer, executor.

PEART, John,

HUDSON, Nathaniel, scrivener, and

PARKER, William, are witnesses.

Proved at London 26 July, 1655, by the executor named, the testator having died at Virginia.

In the Principal Probate Registry, London.

P.C.C. 392 AYLETT.

1654, Nov. 21.

COOPER, John, of Weston Hall, [Warwick], his will names his brother Timothy COOPER now in New England, and his children. " My sister Dorcas." My wife sole executrix.

HALE, Humphrey, and

BUTTERY, John, to be helpful to my wife.

SUTTON, John, witness.

Proved at London 1 Oct. 1655, by Elizabeth COOPER, the relict and executrix named.

From the Records of the Drapers' Company, London.

A.D.
c. 1654. " In Virginia."
BANKS, James, son of Thomas, of London, tailor (? citizen and merchant-taylor) apprenticed 15 April, 1646, to
AMIES, Thomas, for nine years; father bound in £200; made free of the Company 2 Aug. 1654.

In the Principal Probate Registry, London.

P.C.C. 196 AYLETT.

A.D.
1655 (date of proof).
BIRKENHEAD, Isaak, adjutant-general, America, his will names " my nephew Tom "; my nephew Randolph BIRKENHEAD.
SCOTT, Mr Richard, secretary to his Excellency.
VENABLES, General Robert & his son Mr Thomas V.
RUDYARD, Quarter Master General John.
BULLER, Colonel.
John RUDYARD & Richard SCOTT are witnesses. (No date.)
Admon. 29 Sept. 1655, to Randolph BIRKENHEAD, the nephew.

In the Principal Probate Registry, London.

P.C.C. 432 PELL.

1655, July 29.

PLOWDEN, Sir Edmund, kn⁺., of Wanstead, co. Southampton, "knight, Lord Earl Palatine and Captain Generall of the Province of New Albion in America and a peere of the Kingdome of Ireland," in his will desires to be buried " in Lidbury church in Shropshire in the chappell of the PLOWDENS neere Plowden," with arms, inscription and brass plates of my eighteen children with " my perfect pedigre as is drawne at my house." He refers to his eldest son Francis & his (Sir Edmund's) wife, " undutifull and unnaturall practises and carriage . . . he having married a woman of mean parentage called Margaret."

MARRINER, M⁺ Peter, my wife's father. My daughter Winifred P. My son Thomas his daughter and Thomazin his wife. My brother Francis and his son Edmund P.

CARTER, Anne, wife of . . . CARTER in Berkshire, daughter of

JAMES, Thomas, of Burfeild.

LAKE, Dame Ann, my sister.

SHARPE, Henry, my late servant, sole executor.

HALL, Benedict, Esq., my kinsman, overseer.

MASON, Sir William, of Gray's Inn, knight, a trustee, for this my plantation . . . my province of New Albion. My undertakers to transport thither a number of men (as follows)

MONSON, Lord, fifty.

SHERRARD, Lord, a hundred.

DANBY, Sir Thomas, a hundred.

BATTS, Captaine, his heire, a hundred.

ELTONHEAD, M⁺, a Master in Chancery, fifty.

ELTONHEAD, his eldest brother, fifty.

BOWLES, M⁺, late Clarke of the Crowne, forty.

CLEYBOURNE, Captain, in Virginia, fifty, and many others in England, Virginia and New England.

SMITH, Will., R. MINSHULL, Gilbert JONES, Geo. PENNE are witnesses at Albion.

Proved at London 27 July, 1659, by Henry SHARPE.

In the Principal Probate Registry, London.

P.C.C. 256 BERKELEY.

1655, Sept. 8.

LUDLOWE, George, of the county and parish of Yorke in Virginia, Esquire, his will names my nephew Thomas, eldest son to my brother Gabriell L., Esq., deceased. My sixteenth part of the ship " Mayflower " whereof
WHITE, Captain William, is commander, which part I bought of
HARWAR, Mr Samuel, of London, merchant, at the Sunne & Harp in Milk Street.
My now wife Elizabeth LUDLOWE. My brother Roger LUDLOWE'S children.
ALVEN, Mr William, of London, merchant, and
CRAY, Mr John, that lives at the Greene Man on Ludgate Hill, overseers.
BUSHRODE, Mr Thomas.
LANGRISH, Samuel, my cosin.
BERNARD, George, son to Colonel William B.
WEBSTER, George, son to Capt. Richard W., of James Towne.
BOWLER, M^r, the tanckard he brought in.
GOOCH, Major William.
WARNER, Capt. Augustine.
WALDRON, Doctor Henry.
GREEHAM, Jane, my servant.
HURST, Mrs Rebecca, whom my nephew Thomas intends to marry.
TROTT, Nicholas, and
HODGES, Augustus, are witnesses.

Codicil: My nephew Jonathan LUDLOWE, eldest son to my brother Roger, who lives in Ireland at Dublin, to be executor if Thomas marries Mrs. Rebecca HURST. 23 Oct. 1655.

BIDDLECOMBE, James, witness.

Admon. 1 Aug. 1656, to Roger LUDLOWE, Esq., the father and curator to Jonathan, Joseph, Roger, Anne, Mary and Sarah LUDLOW, minors, the nephews & nieces and " residuarie legataries " as to deceased's estate in England.

In the Principal Probate Registry, London.

P.C.C. 233 BERKELEY.

1655, Sept. 24.

WESTHROPE, John, of London, marchant, in his will gives " to the Church of Martimber in Virginia two thousand pounds of marchantable Tabacco . . . towards the repaireing or the building up of a new Church for divine worship . . . A communion cupp, my great Bible and a book called Bishopp Andrewes Sermons both in my house in Virginia." He names
SADLER, Master John, my father.
COOPER, Thomas, son of Walter in the Mayne neer James Town.
CLARKE, Joshua, my servant by Indenture.
SMITH, Thomas, my servant.
BECKFORD, Anne, my sister, wife of Edmond, gent.
HENSHAW, Frances, my sister, wife of Edward, gent.
BICKERTON, Bridget, my sister, wife of Richard.
GIBSON, Dorothy, my sister, wife of Marke.
READE, Captain Abraham, master of "The Seaven Sisters."
THOMAS, Judeth, my sister, wife of William.
 Edward HENSHAW, gent., and Edmond BECKFORD, gent., executors.
HENSHAWE, Tho.,
CRAKE (? DRAKE), Joseph, and
OVERINGE, Robert, are witnesses.
 Proved at London 12 June, 1656, by the executors named.

In the Parish Registers of St. Olave, Hart street, London.

1655, Oct. 1.

LINSFORD, John, son of Elizabeth, bapt.; born in New England 31 March, 1651.

In the Principal Probate Registry, London.

P.C.C. 455 BERKELEY.

1655, Oct. 6.

SHAWE, John " pertaininge unto the good Friggott called The Glocester, under the command of
BLAKE, Admirall, now in America, in his will names " my father William SHAWES now living in Noathshills in countie of Northumberland."
THEW, Cuthbeard, executor.
LANES, Robert,
DRYWOOD, Daniel, and
LOCKE, John, scribe, are witnesses.
Proved at London 1 Dec. 1656 by the executor named.

In the Principal Probate Registry, London.

P.C.C. 175 BERKELEY.

1655, Oct. 31.

MERIMAN, George, citizen and cooper of London, in his will names " my sonne Nathaniell MERRIMAN now resident in New England "; son John executor.
NORMAN, Elizabeth, my daughter, wife of Master John NORMAN.
ALLISON, Henry, my servant, apprentice.
LOVE, William,
TURGIS, Richard, and
FIFETT, Richard, are witnesses.
Proved at London 19 May 1656 by the executor named.

In the Principal Probate Registry, London.

P.C.C. 427 BERKELEY.

A.D.
1656 (date of proof).
MARTYN, Nicholas, late of Ratcliffe, Middlesex, but deceased coming from Virginia, in his will names
FARTHINGE, Mary. "I give her all my estate whatsoever."
WATSON, John, and
ROYDON, George, are witnesses. (No date.)
Admon. 25 Nov. 1656, to Mary FARTHING.

In the Principal Probate Registry, London.

P.C.C. 249 RUTHEN.

1656, Feb. 19.
LLOYD, Elizabeth, of Elizabeth River in Lower Norffolke in Virginia, widow, in her will names
LAMBERT, Lt-Col. Thomas, 2000 lbs. of tobacco. To Rachel his daughter £5 to pay her passage to Virginia.
DAVIES, Mr William.
SHIPP, Mr William.
PINNER, Mr Richard, his son, my godchild.
SAYERS, Mr, his son, my godchild.
SANDERSON, Mr
MATTS, James, of Bristoll.
HART, Mr Nicholas, looking after my business in Virginia.
EAVANS, Mary, my sister, wife of Thomas EAVANS of Kilkenny in Ireland, gent., executor.
COLLINS, Dr, of Bristoll, to be paid.
PYNER, Willi,
MANSFIELD, Jane, Sara MATTS and James MATTS are witnesse.
Proved at London 15 June 1657, by the executor named.

In the Principal Probate Registry, London.

P.C.C. 346 BERKELEY.

1656, April 9.
READ (REED), William, of Newcastle on Tine, in his will names " my wife and four youngest children." George, Ralph, and Abigail my children married in New England.
BRENTON, Mr William, in New England owes me £60.
KILLINGWORTH, M^r, £20.
THEATON, Marke, of Black Cullerton, £30.
HALL, Mrs Flora, £20.
WALKER, Anthony, £12.
OALES, M^r
ERINGTON, George, of Lough house, and his son in law.
ANDERSON, Gowan.
CHICKEN *alias* WATSON, Mary.
CUTTER, William, and
GIBSON, Thomas, are witnesses.
Admon. 31 Oct. 1656 to Mabell READ, widow, the relict.

In the Public Record Office, London.

CHANCERY DEPOSITIONS BEFORE 1714.

COKE *v.* BISSON.

1657, Sept. 1.
COKE, John, *versus*
BISSON, William, and
WHITE, John.
WILLIAMSON, William, deposes that 17 months before the Assize at Dorchester [Dorset] in 1636 he was in Boston, New England, where he saw
BAUTON, Ambrose, an apothecary, about 52 years of age, who said he was from the West part of England. [Query, son of Nicholas BAUTON, born at Shilling Okeford, Dorset, in 1602, apprenticed to his uncle Ambrose BAUTON of London, apothecary, and died *c*. 1637.—*Somerset & Dorset Notes & Queries*, 18/262.]

In the Principal Probate Registry, London.

P.C.C. 450 PELL.

1659, June 25.

JOHNSON, Luke, of Virginia, planter, his will names his wife Anne.
TURTON, John, my uncle, of West Bromwich, Stafford, gent., and
CARIE, James, citizen and salter of London, (executors) & Elizt^h his wife.
BANESTER, Mr John, and Elizabeth his wife, and John, my god son, son of John B., of Yorke River in Virginia, planter.
BRYEN, Robert, son of Robert B., of Virginia, planter.
MORTON, Richard, and
STEDMAN, Peter, servant to
RUSSELL, Thomas, scrivener, are witnesses.
Proved at London 1 August 1659 by the executors named.

From the Records of the Drapers' Company, London.

1664, March 15.

BURNHAM, John, son of Rowland, of Virginia, America, deceased, apprenticed to William PARKER for eight years.
JEFFERIES, John, of London.
COLCLOUGH, Thomas, citizen and grocer, and
BURNHAM, Thomas, of London, gent., bound in £500.

From the Acts of the Privy Council, England.

No. 661.

1665, July 5, Whitehall.

A number of convicted Quakers in the county gaol of Hertford are to be transported to some of His Majesty's plantations, "excepting Virginia and New England," in "The Nicholas" of London.

GATES, Captain
LUCAS, Nicholas
PRYER, Francis
FEAST, Henry
MARSHALL, Henry
BLINDALL, John
TREYHERNE, Samuel
HERNE, Jeremiah
CROOKE, Robert
FAIRMAN, Robert
THOMAS, Richard
BRESTBONE, John
STENT, Henry
LAWNDEY, Lewis
MESSE, Thomas

BURR, William & Thomas
HART, Robert
SWEETING, Henry
LARKIN, William
WHITTENBURY, Mary
WOLLESTONE, Samuel
CRAWLEY, Thomas
PARKIN, Edward
WITHAM, John
ADAMS, William
DAY, John
THORROWGOOD, John
DEANE, Jeremiah
PICKET, John
FAIRMAN, William

At Taunton Castle, Somerset.

SOMERSET ARCH. SOC. DEEDS—"VARIOUS," BOX NO. 2.

1666, Aug. 10.

DANIELL, Henry, marchant of Bristol, protests against refusal of SANDERS, William, haberdasher, Bristol, to honour a bill as follows, ROGERS, William (Signs) "Virginia, 3 May 1666, pay CARY, Col. Milles, £3 17s. for Virginia import and cocquett money for 37 hogsheads Virginia tobacco, 6 May, 1666, pay to Henry DANIELL or order. Milles CARY"
HARTWELL, Thomas, notary public, Bristol. (Signs.)

In the Principal Probate Registry, London.

P.C.C. 179 PENN.

1670, Nov. 9.

PHIPPS, John, citizen and clothworker of London, names his wife Elizabeth. "My sonne Henry PHIPPS now in Mary land in the parts beyond the seas," executor.

WICKS, Mr Michaell, my landlord, and
LEE, Mr Godfrey, executors in trust.

Admon. 3 Dec. 1670, to Elizabeth, the relict, in the absence of Henry, the son.

Proved at London 15 Oct. 1673, by Henry the son.

In the Principal Probate Registry, London.

P.C.C. 161 KING.

1676, March 16.

HITCHINS, Samuel, of Allhallows Barking, citizen & draper of London, in his will names "my two nephews David & Joseph, sons of my brother David HITCHINS, who are now living in New England near Boston."

In the Registers of St Martin Outwich, London.

1676, March 19.

WEST, John, son of Edward and Martha, inhabitant on ye River of Piscataque in New England, bapt.

In the Principal Probate Registry, London.

COMMISSARY OF SURREY.

33 CHAPMAN.

1681, April 1.
NEVINSON, Roger, rector of Hambledon, Surrey, his will names
BURROW, Anne, of Hambledon, wife of Arnold BURROW.
HEDGER, Jeremy, his widow.
BILLINGHURST, Francis, of Hambledon, husbandman, my late servant.
NEVINSON, John, of Water Towne in New England, my loving sonne.
DOVER, Mary, George, Elizabeth & Prudence, the children of my daughter Elizabeth DOVER, deceased.
MARTER, Miles, of Great Bookham, my son in law, his children Thomas, Miles & Jane.
FLEMING, John, Sarah, & Mary, executors.
BETTSWORTH, Thomas, of Godalming, yeoman, overseer.
SMITH, Sarah,
MILLS, Francis, and
MONGER, Jo., are witnesses.
Proved 28 April 1681, by John FLEMING, and 15 Feb., 1683, by Sarah FLEMING, John having died. Power reserved for Mary FLEMING.

In the Principal Probate Registry, London.

P.C.C. ADMONS.

1682, March 2.
CROSSE, William, of Blandford, Dorset, died in Maryland. Administration granted to
DRAPER, Richard, the principal creditor.

In the Principal Probate Registry, London.

COMMISSARY OF SURREY.

BOOK "CHAPMAN," FO. 42.

1682/3, Jan. 15.

MILLOWES, Elizabeth, of St Olave's, Southwark, Surrey, widow, "aged and weake," in her will names

WELLS, Thomas, "my son, who went into parts beyond seas to Maryland or other partes in America or elsewhere, when he shall come and arrive into England."

PARKER, John, my son in law, of Crusifix Lane, St Olave, Southwark, feltworker, the husband of my daughter Mary, executor.

WHITWORTH, Jeremiah,

CANTON, Margarett,

TUDER, Jno., scrivener, next Dogg Taverne neare Billingsgate, are witnesses.

Proved 15 Feb. 1682/3, by John PARKER.

In the Public Record Office, London.

CHANCERY B AND A BEFORE 1714.

COLLINS 433/20.

HORE *v.* DEVENISH.

1683, Dec. 2.

DEVENISH, John, son of Peter D., of Holy Trinity parish, Dorchester, Dorset, by Elizabeth his wife, believed to be still living in Virginia, for Elizabeth DEVENISH, his sister had lately received a letter from him. The other sister of John DEVENISH was

HORE, Mary, wife of George, of Kilmington, Somerset, who sued his sister-in-law Elizabeth in this suit.

(*Somerset & Dorset N. & Q.*, 19/222.)

In possession of the late F. A. Crisp.

MARRIAGE SETTLEMENTS.

1686, Oct. 28.

SHERWOOD, George, of Bushby, Leic., gent., his second son Sampson, citizen and draper of London, and

PARKE, Jane, of Stepney, Middlesex, spinster, youngest daughter of Daniel, late of Virginia, Esq., deceased.

PERRY, Micajah, (Signs.)

LANE, Thomas, of London, merchants

SHERWOOD, John, of London, grocer. (Signs.)

Intended marriage of Sampson SHERWOOD and Jane PARKE. George SHERWOOD grants to PERRY, &c., "Hassocke" and "Doveland," and "Foster's Close" in Thurnby, Leic., to the use of Sampson and Jane and their issue.

HABERFIELD, Edward,

MAWSON, Richard & Charles, are witnesses.

In the Public Record Office, London.

CHANCERY BILLS AND ANSWERS BEFORE 1714.

MITFORD 350/197.

HOLMAN *v.* PITT.

1687, Feb. 25.

HOLMAN, Samuel, late of New England and now of Weymouth and Melcombe Regis, Dorset, merchant, brother & heir of John H. of Jamaica, merchant, (died May 1670), and son of Arthur H., of Weymouth, &c. A messuage, &c., in Maiden Street, Weymouth, conveyed in trust in 1638 or 1639 to his intended wife,

WILLIAMS, Eleanor, dau. of Robert W., of Shetterton in Bere Regis, Esq. She died in March 1686.

HOLMAN, Arthur abovenamed had by Eleanor, the said John, Samuel and Arthur, and three daughters, Sarah, Mary & Amye, all now dead. He died about 1651.

PITT, Mathew, merchant, is def[t].

In the Principal Probate Registry, London.

COMMIS. SURREY.

BOOK "CHAPMAN," FO. 63.

1689, April 19.
PEAKE, Richard, of St Saviour's, Southwark, Surrey, gentleman, in his will names
HILL . . . my brother & sister, living in Whetstone near Tidson in the county of Derby, to whom £10 and one gold ring of the posie "Memento me, G.P. obt. 8 Jan. 76," &c.
PEAKE, Robert & William, my kinsmen at Whetstone.
ARMSTRONGE, James.
SEELE, Elizabeth, my daughter in law, under 17.
KNOWLES, Edward, my friend, of St Olave's, Southwark, scrivener.
FARRELL, Neale, my friend, a gold ring of the posie "Not the value but my love."
PEAKE, Anne, my loving wife, to whom all my estate in the Island of Virginia, executrix.
Proved 4 May, 1689 by the executrix named.

In Blandford Probate Registry.

ARCHD. OF DORSET.

NO. 15, 1693.

1692, Oct. 7. Will of
BILES, Dorothy, widow, of All Saints, Dorchester, names "my son William in Pennsylvania or elsewhere and his children, my son Charles in Pennsylvania or elsewhere and his children, and my son Jonathan in New England or elsewhere."
Proved 25 May, 1693.

In the Principal Probate Registry, London.

P.C.C. ADMONS. 1695.

FO. 51.

1695, March 23.
GRAY, Grace, of Symondsbury, Dorset, deceased. Administration to
KEMBLE, Grace, wife of John, now in Virginia, the daughter.

In the Principal Probate Registry, London.

P.C.C. 36 ASH.

1702, July 23.
MEAD, William, late of the Island of Nevis, America, and now of London, Esquire, in his will mentions
SMITH, Daniel, and
CARPENTER, Henry, his friends in America.

In Blandford Probate Registry.

ARCHD. OF DORSET.

NO. 19, 1704.

1704, Aug. 5. Will of
FOY, Edith, widow, of All Saints, Dorchester, names "my son James FOY, now dwelling in New England."
Proved 25 Sept. 1704.

In the Principal Probate Registry, London.

P.C.C. 82 PRICE.

1711, June 21.
DUNTON, John, citizen and stationer of London, of St Giles, Cripplegate, in his will names
WILKINS, Richard, of Boston, New England, " my antient Landlord," and his daughter Comfort WILKINS. " When I lived in New England."
BRICK, M^{rs}, " Living at Boston, New England, and was a widow while I lived there."
COOKERILL, Mr Thomas, " embarked to America," and many others.
Admon. 27 June, 1744, to a creditor.

In the Principal Probate Registry, London.

P.C.C. 184 LEEDS.

1711/12, Feb. 23. Will of
BROWNE, Peregrine, of the city of London, merchant, names "all those my Plantations in Maryland called Turkey Point and Ratcliffe Crosse," to wife Margaret (executrix).
My children Peregrine, Joseph, John, Margaret and
DUDDLESTONE, Elizabeth.
BROCKE, Mr Joseph, my father in law, to be overseer.
KENNETT, Wh.,
NOTTINGHAM, John,
KILNER, Tho., are witnesses.
Proved 10 Aug. 1713, by Margaret BROWNE, the executrix named.
Admon. 30 Sept. 1712, to Peregrine BROWNE, sen^r., of the goods of Peregrine BROWNE, jn^r., who died in Maryland, a bachelor (fo. 172).
Admon. 17 Oct. 1713, to Margaret BROWN, widow, the relict & executrix of Peregrine BROWN, sen^r., the father & administrator of the goods, &c., of Peregrine BROWN, jn^r., late of Maryland in America, now also deceased. (fo. 225.)

Parish Register of St Dunstan's, Stepney, Middx.

1692, Dec. 25. Peregrine BROWNE of Ratcliffe, mariner, and Margaret BROCK, married.

In the Public Record Office, London.

EXCHEQUER DEPOSITIONS.

1 GEO. I, MICH. 39.

1714, May 21.
CARROLL, Charles, *versus*
STEVENS, Joseph.
Actions at law 20 years ago in the law courts of Maryland, against the def^t. by
LYNES, Philip.
Copies of proceedings of the said Courts.

In the Fleet Registers, London.

VOL. 26.

1716, Oct. 12.
STEPHENS, Robert, of New England, sayler, bachelor, and
BAYLEY, Anne, of Deptford, widow, married.

In the Public Record Office, London.

CHANCERY PROCEEDINGS, 1714–58.

CARTER *v.* DOVE, 30/12.

A.D.
1719. CARTER, Samuel, and Mary his wife, widow of
GOODMAN, Robert, and only child of
STAWELL, Robert, of Exeter, gent., deceased, and Elizabeth his wife.

versus

DOVE, Francis, and Rebecca, his wife, widow of
LAHORNE, Arthur, of New England, deceased.
Will of the said STAWELL, a Lieutenant in the Marines, who died in New England, brother of John STAWELL.

In the Public Record Office, London.

CHANCERY PROCEEDINGS, 1714–58.

CARTER *v.* WISE, 1710/2 AND 25.

A.D.
1720. CARTER, Robert, of Lancaster County, Virginia, Esq., *versus*
WISE, Thomas and Robert.
SANDFORD, Thomas, and
SANDWELL, James, of London, merchants.
The plaintiff possessed of several tobacco plantations. Claim to payment for tobacco consigned by plaintiff to defendants.

From the Records of the Drapers' Company, London.

1720, March 30.
SMITH, William, son of Joseph, of Virginia, "mercator," apprenticed to James LARKES for seven years.

In Wells Probate Registry.

BISHOPS COURT, NO. 44, 1723.

c. 1723. Will of
FRY, Jane, of Crewkerne (Somerset), mentions husband Joshua FRY and son Joshua FRY.
[Refers to Col. Joshua FRY (son of Joshua and Jane FRY of Crewkerne), of William and Mary College, who died 31 May, 1754, on the Potomac River.—*Somerset and Dorset Notes and Queries*, 18/263.]

In the Principal Probate Registry, London.

P.C.C. 76 WAKE.

1731, April 29.

BRANSTONE, William, of Sonning, Berks, yeoman, in his will names " my kinsman William BRANSTONE of Pensilvania his three daughters " and others.
Proved 23 April, 1737.

In the Principal Probate Registry, London.

P.C.C. 198 PRICE.

1733, April 22.

GRAPE, James, of New Windsor, Berks, gentleman, in his will names his eldest son Richard, son James, daughters Esther and Arabella, son Samuel, now in South Carolina, grand-dau. Mary, under 21.
SALE, Revd John,
WATERSON, William, and
SADLER, Elliot, my friends.
HOBBS, Thomas,
RICHARDSON, Nathill, and
SUMNER, William, are witnesses.
Proved 18 July, 1733.

In the Principal Probate Registry, London.

P.C.C. 184 EDMUNDS.

1733, July 27.

LLOYD, John, of Sarphley in the Province of South Carolina his will names wife Sarah, 640 acres on Wattamaw r̃ brother Thomas, 2000 acres on Four Hole Swamp, my half-brothers David, Richard, Edward and Hugh LLO the family pictures hanging in my front parlour.

GRIFFITH, *alias* MOSTYN, Jane, my cousen.

IZARD, Ralph, and

WAREING, Benjamin, Esq^{rs}, and my wife executors.

JENYS & BAKER, from whom I bought a negro girl, Maria.

WALKER, Mr Richard, on the broad path leading to

THOROWGOOD'S plantation, and to

HUME, Mr Robert, his plantation.

PRIOLEAU, Samuel

MOULTRIE, Jno.

BALLYNTINE, John, and

LEWIS, Jno., are witnesses.

Codicil, 26 Sept. 1733. My house, &c., in Charles Town.

MOULTRIE, Jno.

RUSSELL, Joseph, and

LLOYD, Edward, are witnesses.

Second codicil. My lots in the town of Childsbury, 28 Sept. 173;

AKIN, Eliz., jun^r.

RUSSELL, Joseph, and

STEERS, Thomas, are witnesses.

Third codicil. 19 Oct. 1733.

STEERS, Thomas

THOMAS, Rachel, and

AKIN, Eliz., jun^r, are witnesses.

CHAMPNEYS, Jno., dep. secretary, certifies.

Admon. 7 June, 1746, to John NICKELSON, administrator of John LLOYD, an infant, deceased, the only son, for the benefit of Sarah LLOYD, an infant, sister of the said infant, the executors having died. Testator late of Sarphley in the parish of St James, Goose Creek, in Berkeley County, South Carolina.

In the Principal Probate Registry, London.

CONSIST. OXON.

1734, Sept. 10. Will of
ABRAHAM, William, of Sherburn, Oxon., gent., names "my son William ABRAHAM in Boston, New England, son Woodward ABRAHAM of Berkhamsted and his daughters, son Benjamin of Ashby de la Zouch, kinsman Thomas CURTES of Wapping."
YEOMANS, John & James, my grandsons.
Proved at Oxford 21 Oct. 1734.
[The will of William ABRAHAM of Charlestown, Mass., distiller, dated 18 Aug. 1763 ; proved 17 Sept. 1763, wife Martha, children William, Woodward, Martha, Elizabeth and Nathaniel, and dau. Mary BOYLSTON, deceased. Probate Registry, Middlesex, Mass.]

In the Principal Probate Registry, London.

P.C.C. 47 DUCIE.

1734/5, Jan. 30. Will of
COX, William, of Park Mill, Somerset, names
FRY, Mr Joshua, and
KENNY, Captain William, my two friends in Virginia.
[*See* under date 1723.]

From the Records of the Drapers' Company, London.

WARDENS' MINUTES.

1737, Sept. 14.
SWAIN, Richard, of the Green Coat School (Greenwich), age about 16 years, to have £5 to place him apprentice to
GRIFFIN, James, of Boston, in New England, merchant.

In H.M. General Register House, Edinburgh.

COMM. EDINBURGH.

1738, May 25.
LAING, William, of Freehold in Monmouth, New Jersey, died ——. He was oeconymist in the King's College, Aberdeen, 1685, when his brother George, in Langside, gave him a Bond for £39. James LAING in Kirktown of Fetter Angus, son of said George. George LAING, deceased, merchant in Old Aberdeen, own brother of said William, and father of
CHALMERS, Barbara, wife of William, writer in Edinburgh.

In H.M. General Register House, Edinburgh.

COMM. EDINBURGH.

1739, Jan. 9.
SCOTT, Mr Alexander, rector of Overworlton, Stafford County, on river Potomac, Virginia, died 1 April, 1738. Inventory by George SCOTT, writer in Edinburgh, the brother german.
OSWALD, Richard, & Co., merchants in Glasgow, owe £12 for four hogsheads of tobacco sent them in October, 1737.

From an Abstract of Title to premises in Paulton, Somerset, in possession of George SHERWOOD.

1740, April 15 and 16.
COOMBE, Joseph, of Plumsted, co. Bucks, Pennsylvania, cordwainer, and Sarah his wife, eldest son and heir of Elizabeth COOMBE, deceased, daughter and heir of
HILL, John, and Elizabeth his wife, both deceased, parties to indentures as to premises in Paulton.

From printed Law Reports, Chancery.

ATK. 2/254.

YOUNG *v.* PEACHY.

A.D.
1741 Fox, Margaret, wife of Joseph, and her husband went to South Carolina after 1726, " to secrete themselves from their creditors." He died in Aug. 1735, and she in 1735, without issue, intestate. She had a sister

YOUNG, Lydia, wife of . . . YOUNG, married 1726, now plaintiff; both were daughters of

BREEDON, Zaccheus, who died in March, 1734, son of Sir Robert BREEDON.

In the Principal Probate Registry, London.

P.C.C. 85 POTTER.

1741, April 3.

WHITE, Limpany, in his will, made in " Catragine Harbour," names his sisters Katherhine & Martha WHITE, brother Maurice WHITE, and

DURON, Katherhine, widow, of Second River in the Province of New East Jersey in North America. (No witnesses.) On 5 March, 1746, Rev. Edmond WHITE of Tooting Graveney, Surrey, clerk, and David LONG of St Andrew, Holborn, Middlesex, yeoman, testified to the handwriting of the deceased, late Lieutenant of the Reg^t of Foot commanded by Col. William GOOCH, Esq.

Admon. 5 March, 1746, to Martha WHITE, spinster; the deceased having died at Carthagena in the West Indies, a bachelor.

In the Principal Probate Registry, London.
P.C.C. 59 EDMUNDS.

1742, April 20.

POPE, James, of the Island of Madeira, merchant, in his will names wife Margaret, two houses on the bridge at Bristol.

BARRETT, John, native of Brosley (? Broseley, Salop). My sister Susannah B., at Brosley.

POPE, Francis, of Rhode Island, my cousin, my estate of the Manachty in Wales.

BECKFORD, Mr Thomas, merchant in London, executor with my nephew John BARRETT.

Admon. 6 Feb. 1745, to Thomas BECKFORD.

Proved at London 20 Feb. 1746, by Thomas BECKFORD on the death of John BARRETT, Esq.

Admon. 18 July, 1851, to James Davison WADHAM, administrator of the goods, &c., of John BARRETT, the nephew.

In the Principal Probate Registry, London.
P.C.C. 262 EDMUNDS.

1742, Sept. 1.

HAYNES, Thomas, "of the county of Warwick," [Virginia], in his will names his son William, lands on this side Stony Creek bought of Stephen EVANS, between Wills River and the Rockey Run, the Hickmas Line; son Thomas. Marriage agreement 11 Jan. 1739. Plantation called Myer's and Price's. Grandson Herbert HAYNES, son of my son Anthony. Prince George County; son Richard; White Oak swamp bought of Robert MOODY. Son Andrew HAYNES. Mr KEITH's line, Notway Road, Wills Run; bought of Theophilus FIELD. My lot in York Town; land bought of William CARY, jun^r. My daughters Martha & Mary. Martha, daughter of my son Herbert HAYNES, deceased. My wife Martha. My mother living.

CARY, Elizabeth, my daughter.

HAYNES, Ann, Elizabeth, and Laurence are witnesses.

Admon. 27 Sept. 1746, to James WILKES, attorney of Andrew HAYNES, now residing in Virginia.

From Stinsford Parish Register, Dorset.

1742, Dec. 17.
    APPLEBEE, Benjamin, of New York, was buried.

In the Principal Probate Registry, London.

                P.C.C. 318 EDMUNDS.

1743, March 22.
    BRADLEY, Edward, of the city of Philadelphia in the province of Pennsylvania, glazier, in his will names his wife Esther, my negroe slaves York, Daphne and the child Gin. Brothers Thomas & Joseph BRADLEY and William his son. Effects in Great Britain.
    KINNERSLEY, Ebenezer, and
    LEACH, Thomas, both of the same city, shopkeepers, executors with wife.
    HAW, William, land lately sold to.
    HOWARD, Thomas, of whom I took a stable.
    STRETTLE, Robert, and
    SHED, George, their messuages and lots in Front street.
    CARPENTER, Joshua, his rent charges in Elbow lane.
    SHEPHERD, Ann, my sister, & Edward her son.
    TURNER, Pr.
    BROCDEN, C., and Robt. STRETTLE are witnesses.
    Proved at London 8 Nov. 1746, by Edward SHEPHERD; power reserved for William BRADLEY.

In the Principal Probate Registry, London.
P.C.C. 121 POTTER.

1743, March 29.
COOK, Edmund, of the Island of Maryland, in his will names hi‑ brothers Simon and Robert, sisters Abigail and Elizabeth Estate of Leasingham near Hempstead in Norfolk.
BROWN, James, of this Island, executor in trust for
MARTIN, Charles and Susanna, of the city of Norwich, my cousins executors.
BROWN, Jno.,
SMART, Thos., and
SNOUD, T., are witnesses.
Proved at London 19 May, 1747, by Charles MARTIN ; power reserved for Susanna.

In the Principal Probate Registry, London.
P.C.C. 79 EDMUNDS.

1743, May 16.
CHICHESTER, Richard, of Virginia, in his will names wife Ellen executrix, negroes and horses, estate in England, Fairweather‑ plantation whereon I now live. To son John plantation in Lancaster County called Newsoms. My four daughters Elizabeth, Ellen, Mary and Hannah, under age and unmarried, son Richard.
CARTER, Joseph.
MITCHELL, Robert, and
BALL, Joss, gentlemen, trustees.
CARTER, Joseph and Ann,
LAWRY, Garvin, and
DILLON, Michael, are witnesses.
Admon. 15 March, 1745, to John & Richard TUCKER, Esquires, attorneys of Ellen CHICHESTER.
Admon. 28 May, 1763, to Richard CHICHESTER, the brother & executor of John C., the son.
Admon. 9 June, 1803, to William MURDOCH for the use of Sarah C., widow of Richard, now residing in the county of Fairfax, Virginia.

In the Principal Probate Registry, London.

P.C.C. 354 EDMUNDS.

1743, Nov. 23.

HIGGINS, Nathaniel, of Cape Codd in New England, now mariner on board His Majesty's ship "Torbay," Captain John GAS-COIGNE, commander, in his will names

BROWNE, Thomas, of St Mary, Hackney, Middlesex, "my trusty friend and shipmate," sole executor.

SEARES, Abr^m., and

CRICK, Henry, are witnesses.

Admon. 4 Dec. 1746, of the goods, &c., of the deceased, late of the King's ship "Hornett" sloop, a bachelor, to Sarah BROWNE, widow, attorney of Thomas BROWNE, now on board H.M.S. "Nottingham."

In the Principal Probate Registry, London.

P.C.C. 197 EDMUNDS.

1744, March 13.

AVERY, Joseph, late of Conecticut in New England, but now residing in the city of Bristol, mariner, in his will names

VINCENT, James, of Bristol, clerk.

STONE, Betty, of Bristol, spinster.

DAY, Jane, of Bristol, spinster, sole executrix.

CHURCHMAN, John,

BARTLETT, Ambrose, and

MURRAY, James, are witnesses.

Proved at London 7 July, 1746, by the executrix named.

In the Principal Probate Registry, London.

P.C.C. 314 EDMUNDS.

1744, Nov. 25. At Augusta.
WALKER, Nathan, Ensign in a detachment of H.M.'s forces, Major John CAULFIELD, in the Island of Ratan, which belonged to the late American Regiment of Foot commanded by Col. GOOCH, in his will names
GARDNER, John, merchant, of Rhode Island, my cousin.
JENKINS, Lieut., of the aforesaid detachment, and
CARRE, Lieut., of Brigadier WOFF's Regiment of Marines, executors.
HOPKINS, Francis
COSBY, Alexander, and
BARNETT, John Lenn, are witnesses.
Proved at London 15 Oct. 1746, by Andrew CARRE, the surviving executor.

In the Principal Probate Registry, London.

P.C.C. 9 EDMUNDS.

1745, May 6.
DISON, Charles, "late belonging to H.M.S. 'Hastings,' but now in the hospital at Rochester," Kent, in his will names "my beloved brother Philip DYSON of the Court House in Princess Anne County in Virginia," my cozen John DYSON of Limehouse, Middlesex, gentleman, executor, and my brother Francis DYSON.
REED, Edwd, and
STUBBS, Will., are witnesses.
Proved at London 8 Jan. 1745/6, by John DISON.

In the Principal Probate Registry, London.
P.C.C. 23 EDMUNDS.

1745, Dec. 9.

PIERCE, Tobias, " late of New England, but now of London, marriner " in his will names
BURROWS, John, of St Ann, Middlesex, waterman, and Sarah, his wife, executor and executrix.
HESTER, Joseph, notary publick, and
WOOLGAR, William, his servant, are witnesses.
Proved at London 2 Jan. 1745/6, by Sarah BURROWS; power reserved for John BURROWS.

In the Principal Probate Registry, London.
P.C.C. 176 POTTER.

1745/6, Feb. 27.

FENWICKE, John, " late of the Province of South Carolina," but now of St George's, Hanover Square, Middlesex, in his will names " my kinsman " Robert F., of Lincoln's Inn, Esq. My son Edward, now in South Carolina; late brother Edward F., Esq.; my daughter Sarah.
WHITTINGTON, Isaac, Esq., my son in law.
DELORAINE . . . , my daughter, £1000 ; her late husband.
COMPTON, Thos & Elizabeth, of Audley street, St George parish,
ADAMS, Thomas, servant to Lady DELORAINE, are witnesses.
GIBBES, Col. John, my brother in law, and
RUTLEDGE, Andrew, Esq., both of South Carolina.
GOLIGHTLY, Culcheth, my nephew, of South Carolina.
GIBBES, John, my nephew, under 18, son of late Mr William G.
SCOTT, John, my grandson, under 21.

On 22 July, 1747, George MORLEY of St Clement Danes, Esq., Silvia BRAITHWAITE of St George, Hanover Square, widow, and Andrew PRINGLE of St Margaret Pattens, London, merchant, testified to handwriting.

Proved at London 23 July, 1747, by Elizabeth, Countess Dowager of DELORAINE, the daughter; power reserved to Isaac WHITTINGTON and Edward FENWICKE, Esq^{rs}.

Proved at London 2 Dec. 1749, by Edward FENWICKE, Esqr.

In the Principal Probate Registry, London.

P.C.C. 341 EDMUNDS.

1746, April 5.

WARDEN, William, late of Charles Town, South Carolina, but now of St Mary Matfellon, Whitechapel, Middlesex, mariner, names in his will " my freehold in Charles Town," wife Margaret, and two daughters Elizabeth and Catherine WARDEN.

LEGOE, Mr William, of St Mary, Whitechapel, weaver, and COLEMAN, Mr Stephen, of Wapping Wall, ship chandler, executors.

SMITH, Thos.

FRASER, James, and

BAGLING, Jno. Marmaduke, all of Goodmas Fields, London, are witnesses.

Proved at London 18 Nov. 1746, by William LEGOE ; power reserved for COLEMAN.

In the Principal Probate Registry, London.

P.C.C. 116 POTTER.

1746, May 12.

BERTHON, Isaac, now at London, " born at Chattellerault," 6 August, 1663, in his will names

GALHIE, Mr Stephen, " surgeon and apothecary in Steward street in Spittlefielde and Mary Galhie BERTHON his wife, the daughter or issue of Michael BERTHON my cousin german, now at New York," £10,000.

LE CLERC, Elias, watch case maker in Compton street near Leicester Fields, the issue of my cousin Jane BERTHON, widow of Alexander LE CLERC, living at Amsterdam, £2000.

RIBOT, Francis, a mercer at the sign of The Pearl in New Round Court in The Strand, and to Letissa Ribot BERTHON his wife and my relation in the same degree as Mary GALHEE hereabove, who is her sister £1000, &c., &c.

Codicil 23 Feb. 1746/7.

Proved at London 2 May, 1747, by Claude Aubert Elias LE CLERC, GALHIE and RIBOT, the executors named.

In the Principal Probate Registry, London.

P.C.C. 202 EDMONDS.

1746, May 16.
CLAIBORNE, William, of Virginia, at present in London, merchant, confirms his will made in Virginia.
HANBURY, Mr John, of London, merchant, to be executor in England.
RANDOLPH, Edward, jun^r, and
KEENE, Benj., are witnesses.
Proved at London 17 July, 1746, by solemn affirmation of John HANBURY.

In the Principal Probate Registry, London.

P.C.C. 244 EDMUNDS.

1746, July 24.
PRENTIS, John, of New London, Connecticut, New England, mariner, "at present residing in St Martins in the Fields, Middlesex," in his will names "my estate in this kingdom and in the United Netherlands."
BOWDOIN, Mr William, of Boston, in New England, merchant, "but now residing in St Martin's aforesaid," executor for my wife and children.
RYAN, Margaret
HOPKINS, W^m, and
BOLLEME, W., are witnesses.
Proved at London 5 Aug. 1746, by William BOWDOIN.

In the Principal Probate Registry, London.
P.C.C. 304 POTTER.

1746, Aug. 28.

CURRIE, Ebenezer, "of the province of Pensilvania in America, at present in London," in his will gives
GROVES, John, my servant, 100 guinas.
CURRIE, Revd John, of Kinglassie, my father, and Jean my mother
MCALL, Mr Samuel, senior, of Philadelphia, and
SETON, Mr John, of London, merchants, executors.
ELLIOT, Andrew, and
SETON, Andrew, are witnesses.
Proved at London 2 Dec. 1747, by John SETON.

In the Principal Probate Registry, London.
P.C.C. 321 POTTER.

1746, Nov. 4.

ORPWOOD, Mary, of St Margaret, Westminster, Middlesex, spinster, in her will names a "legacy of £100 left me by my grandfather Edmond ORPWOOD of Phillidelphia."
COLLINS, Mary, daughter of William and Elinor C., of East Hanney, Berks, spinster, executrix.
BAKER, Eliz., wife of Thomas BAKER of London.
POMEROY, Richard, of London, gentleman.
KNOWLES, Francis, & John of said place, executors of said Edmond ORPWOOD.
RAKE, Mary,
MALBONE, Mary, and
FINLAYSON, Joanah, are witnesses.
Admon. 15 Dec. 1747, to William COLLINS, father of Mary COLLINS, a minor, under 17.

In the Public Record Office, London.
CHANCERY BILLS AND ANSWERS 1714–58.
MITFORD 2199.
FRY *v.* TRENT.

A.D.
1747. FRY, John, of Bristol, gent., was in Charleston, South Carolina, this year.

In the Principal Probate Registry, London.

P.C.C. 302 POTTER.

1747, April 1.

BURRINGTON, John, of St George, Hannover Square, [Middlesex] in his will gives

CARY, Esquire, gentleman, of St James's, Westminster, "all my estate scituated and lying upon Cape Fear River in North Carolina," sole executor.

BEEKERS, Anna de

MAXWELL, Jane, and

PAGUY, Jean, are witnesses.

Proved at London 14 Dec. 1747, by Esquire CARY, the executor named.

In the Principal Probate Registry, London.

P.C.C. 222 POTTER.

1747, June 4.

BORDLEY, Thomas, "at present of Annaplis in the province of Maryland but intending this day to depart for Great Britain," in his will names "my brother John, our four lots in Annapolis, Augustine manor," brothers Matthias BORDLEY, Stephen & Beale B., and sister Elizabeth B.

WELCH, Mr Wakelin, a debt to.

SMITH, Mrs Margaret, of Mark Lane, London, haberdasher; Mr Martin S., of Mark Lane, executor.

JENINGS, M^r, to assist my executor.

JENINGS, Mary,

YOUNG, B., junior, and

WOODS, Sam., are witnesses.

Proved at London 19 Sept. 1747, by Martin SMITH.

In the Principal Probate Registry, London.

P.C.C. 277 POTTER.

1747, Sept. 22.

DISON, John, of St Ann, Middlesex, gentleman, in his will names "Philip and Francis DISON, of Norfolk Town in Virginia, sons of my late uncle Francis DISON, and their brothers Peter and Pavie DISON." Wife Priscilla. Monthly Meeting of Quakers at Ratcliff.

BAILEY, Sarah, daughter of my Aunt BAILEY, late of Little Moorfields, and her two sisters.

READ, Rodman, late of Chatham, Kent, innholder, his widow, and her seven daughters.

MESSER, Joseph, of Ratcliff, glazier.

SPARROW, Jonathan, of Rotherhithe.

OLLAVE, Joseph, and his brother Thomas.

BESSE, Joseph, my brother in law, and Joseph his son.

GREVILLE, Silvanus, shipwright, executor, with wife and BESSE.

BENTLEY, Sarah, daughter of Joseph BESSE, & wife of Thomas B.

STOCKER, Seymour, and

HEARLE, Thomas, are witnesses.

Proved at London 7 Nov. 1747, by the executors named. Affirmation of Priscilla DISON and Joseph BESSE. [Quakers.]

In the Principal Probate Registry, London.

P.C.C. 253 GREENLY.

1749, Sept. 25.

BENNETT, Richard, of Queen Ann County, Maryland, in his will names his wife Elizabeth, deceased.

PARKER, George, my cousin, of Accomack County, Virginia; estates at Bennett's Creek, Nansemond County.

DULANY, Lloyd, son of Daniel, Esq., by my cousin Henrietta Maria.

HOWELL, Mr John, from whom I purchased The Ponds and Williamstone in Kent County on the eastern side of Steel Pencreck.

HOWARD, Matthew, from whom I purchased land adjoining called Adventure.

DORSEY, Henrietta Maria, and

CHEW, Margaret and Mary, daughters, and Bennet and Philemon, sons of Samuel CHEW, deceased, and Henrietta Maria DULANY.

MACCUBBINS, Mary, my cousin, daughter of

CARROLL, Dr Charles, of Annapolis; her brother John.

NEALE, Edward, my cousin, of Queen Ann's County; his son Edward; his daughter Eleanor by his wife Mary.

LYNCH, John, to whom land sold.

BROWNE, Priscilla, my cousin, wife of Mr Charles; Elizabeth his daughter and sons Charles and Robert.

COURSEY, Mr Arthur, lands called Coursey's choice; Back Wye River.

HOLDING, John.

TILGHMAN, William, my cousin; Edward, son of my sister Ann.

BLAKE, Charles, second son of my cousin John; his sisters Henrietta Maria, Mary and Eleanor.

HAWKINS, Mrs Elizabeth, Wright's Chance purchased of,

BLAKE, John, son of my cousin John Sayer B.; his brother Charles and his sister Henrietta Maria; Philemon B., my cousin.

BROOKES, Ann, my cousin now living with me, sister of Priscilla BROWNE.

PRICE, Andrew, from whom land purchased called Stagwell.

SMITH, Margaret, my cousin, dau. of Capt Richard; her sister Priscilla BROWNE.

SETH, Charles, his sons.

1749, Sept. 25—*cont.*
KENDALL, Thomas, and his wife.
LLOYD, Edward, son, and Elizabeth and Henrietta Maria, daughters of my cousin Edward and Ann. Said cousin Edward, of Talbott County, resid. legatee and sole executor.
GRASON, Sarah, wife of George, my mother's bequest to her.
PAINTER, Nicholas, land conveyed by.
CORNWALLIS, William, his widow, from whom land purchased.
BISHOP, William, who made over to me "Smith's Mistake."
CHAMBERLAINE, James, and his sister Henrietta Maria, my cousins.
ROWLAND, Thomas, his daughters Mary and Elizabeth.
WILSON, Thomas, my godson, son of John, lately from Europe for his education.
DOLVIN, John.
EMORY, John, senior.
KINNIMONT, Ambrose, his widow.
CAMCON, James, the taylor, and his wife.
MILLER, James, of Queen Ann's County, son of John, formerly my overseer.
COX, Andrew, son of Lazarus, deceased.
OSMOND, John, of Talbot County, son of John, deceased; his brother Thomas.
LOOCKERMAN, John, jun^r, son of Mr John L.; Jacob L. of Talbot County, his brother.
UNGLE, Mrs Frances, wife of Mr Robert.
HILL, Mr Clement, of Prince George's County.
NEALE, William, my cousin, of Charles County.
DIGGS, William, my cousin.
WILKINSON, Mr Thomas, of Queen Ann's County.
MINSKIE, The widow, of Annapolis.
PORTER, Dr Richard, of Talbot County.
KEMBLE, John, lands mortgaged to me by.
BUCKANNAN, Mr James, merchant in London, and
BROWNE, Mr Charles, with whom I am concerned in cargoes.
TAYLOR, John, deceased, my overseer, his children; Henry, the smith.
HALL, Dorothy, my cousin, wife of Mr Francis, of Prince George's County.

1749, Sept. 25—cont.
HEATH, Mr James, of Cecil County, land purchased of.
HACK, M^r, his land on the Northern side of Sassafras River.
WHEELER, Elizabeth, my cousin, wife of Mr Ignatius, of Baltimore County.
ROUSBY, John, my cousin, son of John, Esq., late of Calvert County, deceased.
THOMAS, Christopher, tenant of Bennett's Choice, his now wife Mary.
HIGGINS, John, my overseer.
ALL, William, my overseer.
FIELD, Samuel.
KENDALL, Thomas.
IMPEY, Mr George, deceased, of whom land purchased in county Hertford, England.
ANDERSON, Mr William, merchant in London.
DARNAL, Mr Henry, of Portland manor, Ann Arundel C^o., and my cousin Elizabeth his wife; Eleanor and Elizabeth his daughters.
HALL, Francis, of Prince George's County, and my cousin Dorothy his wife.
MELVILLE, David, of Dorchester County, and
SHERWOOD, Daniel, of Talbott County, debtors.
THOMAS, Philip, Esq., executor of Samuel CHEW, sen^r, deceased.
CHEW, Ann and Margaret, daughters of my cousin Henrietta Maria DULANY.
SULLIVANT, Timothy, deceased, his eldest son.
ROWLAND, Thomas, my overseer, at Town Quarter.
PICKETT, Captain, and
BRUCE, Captain, importers of negroes.
WALLACE, Mr John, my partner in an adventure.
BROWNE, Mr Charles.
BARKER, William, of Talbott County.
CALDER, Mr James, to whom land in Chester Town, Kent County; James his son.
BELL, Ann, a little girl, niece of my cousin Ann BROOKES; her sister Priscilla BELL.
GRIFFIN, Edward, my tenant of Poplar Ridge in Talbott County.

1749, Sept. 25—*cont.*
ROBINSON, Alice, in my service.
CLARKE, Mr Thomas, in my service several years.
HALL, Robert, of Talbott County, a debtor.
BARROW, Dr Gilbert, of Talbott County.
ARCHBOLD, Richard ⎫
TUITE, James
WALTERS, Jas.
KNOCK, John   ⎬ witnesses.
TAYLAR, John
FETTERS, James, his mark.
COURSEY, John ⎭
DULANY, D., commissary.

Debts remitted to

GRASON, George	Talbott County.
WARNER, Elizabeth	,,
HAMILTON, John	Queen Ann's County.
EVANS, Elizabeth	Talbott County.
CAMPER, William	Dorchester County.
EVERITT, Henry	Queen Ann's County.
PEARSON, Robert	Talbott County.
BUCKLY, William	,,
JONES, Edmond	,,
COTTON, Alexander	,,
RAGLASS, James	,,
SHEHANE, Bridget	Dorchester County.
HALLFIELD, William	,,
MANSELL, Charles	Queen Ann's County.
HUGHES, Richard	Talbott County.
CONNERLY, Dennis	,,
BATEMAN, Christopher	Kent County.
WATTS, Peter	Queen Ann's County.
FRAMPTON, Robert	Talbott County.
NICHOLSON, John	Queen Ann's County.
BRUFF, Katharine	Dorchester County.
PRICE, Mr Andrew	Queen Ann's County.
HART, Richard	Dorchester County.
HEMES, John	Talbot County.

1749, Sept. 25—cont.

Rock, Dennis	Talbot County.
Sutton, Henry	,,
Cassaway, Robert	,,
Hage, John	,,
Griffen, Thomas	,,
Fenwick, Andrew	Queen Ann's County.
Walker, Charles	Talbot County.
Wrightson, Widow	,,
Cook, Samuel	Queen Ann's County.
Taylor, John, the smith	,,
Buck, William	,,
Ray, Alexander	Talbot County.
Hyatt, Edward	Queen Ann's County.
Sattesfield, William	,,
Hunter, Widow	Kent Island.
Foster, Thomas	Talbot County.
Pratt, Widow	Queen Ann's County.
Storey, Francis	Talbot County.
Price, Henry	Queen Ann's County.
Carslake, Edward	Talbot County.
Millington, Oliver	,,
Barnes, Francis	Kent Island.
Miller, John, of Tully's Neck	Queen Ann's County.
Boyd, William	
Wilson, John, ship carpenter	
Homes, Jos.	Talbot County.
Jones, John Allen	,,
Riddle, Andrew	Queen Ann's County.
Adams, Thomas	,,
Peatt, William	,,
Wrightson, Thomas, sailor in Virginia	
Satterfield, Edward, Benjamin, Jos.	Queen Ann's County.
Caldwall, Andrew	Pokeley.
Allcock, Burton Wood	Dorchester County.
Allduck, Harmanns	New Castle.
Seymour, John	Queen Ann's County.
Hawkins, James	Talbot County.

1749, Sept. 25—*cont.*

CLANSEY, John	Queen Ann's County
GRAHAM, David	,,
EVANS, William	,,
JEFFERYS, George	,,
MORTIMORE, William	Talbot County.
HEWBANCK, Adam	,,
BRUFF, Richard, the sawyer	,,
RANSFIELD, Jos.	,,
JONES, Keziah	Queen's Town.
BENSON, Nic[s]	Talbot County.
GARRETTY, Thomas	Kent County.
BRUFF, James	Talbot County.
GAREY, Jane, widow	,,
BALL, Gerrard	Ann Arundel County
DOBSON, George	Queen Ann's County.
GRIFFIN, Nicholas	,,
MURPHEY, Eleanor	,,
LEE, George	,,
WOOTERS, Richard	Tuckahoe.
WEEDEN, Henry	Kent Island.
MOORE, John	Queen Ann's County.
SEYMOR, John	,,
LANE, Walter & John	,,
KNIGHT, Robert	,,
KELLEY, Edmond, the cooper	,,
PLOWMAN, John	,,
EMORY, Arthur, brother of John	,,
SUTTON, John	Talbot County.
KIRKHAM, Affrica	Queen Ann's County.
LAVERTON, John	Dorchester County.
MURFEY, Thomas, his estate	Queen Ann's County.
HARRIS, Thomas, planter	,,
THOMPSON, James	,,
BROWN, Sarah, widow	Talbot County.
CAMPER, Robert	Queen Ann's County.
JOHNSON, Richard	,,
OLDSON, Andrew	,,

1749, Sept. 25—*cont.*

WEBSTER, Thomas, shipwright	
DOWNES, Edward	Queen Ann's County.
RYAN, William	Talbot County.
SMITH, Edward, the sawyer	,,
SLAUGHTER, Edward	,,
MOORS, William, hireling	
NEWELL (? YEWELL) Solo.	Queen Ann's County.
DAVIDSON, Elizabeth	Talbot County.
MILLER, James, joiner	Queen Ann's County.
PUGH, Meredith, millwright	Talbot County.
FLEMIN, Mary, widow	,,
COOK, Francis	,,
YEWELL, Christopher	Queen Ann's County.
JARMAN, Henry	Talbot County.
BAKER, Daniel	,,
SINKLAR, Charles	,,
MURRAY, Susanna	Annapolis.
CLOAK, Morrice	Queen Ann's County.
YOUNG, John (Tuckahoe)	,,
JONES, Christmas	Talbot County.
FALLOWFIELD, John	Queen Ann's County.
GRAHAM, Terrence	Kent County.
EDMONDSON, William	Talbot County.
FRAZIER, John, the cooper	,,
PATTYSON, John	,,
ATCHESON, John	Queen Ann's County.
LYON, John, weaver	Talbot County.
PROUTE, Capt Joseph	
COLLINS, Henry	
ALLEY, John	Queen Ann's County.
SCOTT, Thomas	
COCKRAINE, James	Talbot County.
EDWARDS, Elizabeth	,,
DELAHUNTY, Daniel	Kent County.
SMITH, Thomas	Queen Ann's County.
RICE, William	Kent County.
BLADES, Edmund, sen^r	Talbot County.

1749, Sept. 25.—*cont.*
MERRIDAY, William — Queen Ann's County
LOWE, Vincent — Talbot County.
WARD, Tho[s] — ,,
MANSFIELD, William — ,,
WHALEY, William — ,,
HIGGINS, Thomas — ,,
WILLEN, Joseph — ,,
CULLEN, John — ,,
GELLEY, James — Queen Ann's County.
LAMBER, Richard, the taylor — ,,
BELL, Jacob — ,,
SWEAT, Virtue, estate of — Talbot County.
TANNER, Thomas — Queen Ann's County.
BURMAN, Richard, and
CARPENTER, Johanna — ,,
JELFE, Thomas
JONES, Lewis, estate of — Talbot County.
SKINNER, William — ,,
ROWNEY, Michael — Kent Island.

Codicil names :
TUITE, M[r] James, of Queen Ann's County.
WILSON, Thomas, my godson.
MOLLINEAUX, Rev[d] M[r] Richard
ARCHBULL, Rev[d] M[r] Richard
FETTERS, James, and
HAY, Alexander, who live with me.
BEESTON, William, of Dorchester County, deceased, his estat. administered by
ADAMS, William, of same.
HOWEL, John, of Kent County, deceased.
BRACE, Elizabeth, wife of M[r] John.
BRICE, John, deputy notary publick, Annapolis.
JENNINGS, Hon. Edward, Esq.

Records of the Drapers' Company, London.

1750, March 29.
    GADSDEN, James, son of Thomas, of Charleston, Carolina, **deceased**, apprenticed to John HARGRAVE, citizen & draper, 7 years. Premium £420.
    [Free of the company 1757 ; warden 1782 ; living 1808.]

In the Public Record Office, London.

EXCHEQUER DEPOSITIONS.

30 GEO. II, MICH. 12.

1750, Aug. 31, &c.
    HART, Abraham, and
    STEAD, William, *versus*
    BUTTS, Thomas, and
    HASTINGS, Henry, attorney general.
        Ship the "Two Brothers" ; sugar.
        Depositions taken at New York.

In the Public Record Office, London.

EXCHEQUER DEPOSITIONS.

30 GEO. II, HIL. 3.

1755, Feb. 18, &c.
    STEVENSON, Dr John, died in Virginia, said to be **father of**
    EVERARD, William, who, with
    WATTS, Hannah, widow, are defendants at the suit of
    EVERARD, Susannah, widow of John E.

In the Public Record Office, London.

EXCHEQUER DEPOSITIONS.

30 GEO. II, MICH. 6.

1756, Nov. 5–9.
SIMON, Isaac, *versus*
PHILPOT, Bryan.
The ship "Elizabeth," American built.
TOWERS . . . and def^t. PHILPOT owners.
ROSS, William, commander.
Voyage in 1751 to Maryland, with convicts.

In the Public Record Office, London.

CHAN. PRO. 1758–1800.

NO. 1002.

HENLEY *v.* TEMPLEMAN.

1760, Nov. 20.
HENLEY, John, now of North Carolina, only son of Peter H. lately deceased, and nephew to the Revd Phocion H., rector of St Andrew's, Blackfriars, London.
Regarding lands at Abbot's Wootton, Dorset.

From printed Law Reports, Chancery.

EDEN 2/107.

FOX *v.* COLLINS.

A.D.
1761. COLLINS, Edward, of Virginia in America, had sisters Sidney (second dau.) who married Nehemia COLLINS, "late of Leominster," Ann, of St Ives, Hunts., a def^t., and
BETHELL, Susan, wife of —— BETHELL. They were children of COLLINS, Thomas, of co. Huntingdon, who had as sister
EVANS . . . wife of . . . EVANS, and mother of Phineas EVANS.
(will 7 Sept. 1759, real estate in Northfleet & Wickford, Essex) and a brother
COLLINS, Robert, whose youngest son Robert had a son, Thomas.
COLLINS, Ann, of Bromyard, Hereford, is youngest daughter of Robert, brother of Thomas, of co. Huntingdon.

Bible entries in possession of the late F. A. Crisp

(Fragmenta Genealogica, XII. 102.)

A.D.
176... SHERMAN, Thomas, born 14 Nov. 1740, married
MUNRO, Margaret Maria, dau. of . . . MUNRO, Esq., of Virginia in America. To whom were born 3 children.
[The above Thomas SHERMAN was son of William SHERMAN, ordnance storekeeper at Hull, by his wife Mary, daughter of Alderman John COLLINGS.]

In the Principal Probate Registry, London.

P.C.C. 103 TREVOR.

1770, April 7. Will of
FRY, James, the younger of Southall, Midd^x., tanner, died at Nottingham, Maryland.
Proved 20 March, 1771.

In the Public Record Office, London.

PORT OF LONDON.

1773, Dec. 11 to 18 (ship " Elizabeth," to Virginia).
HILL, John, aged 24, of London, baker.
SMITH, William, aged 42, of Surrey, taylor.
MORGAN, William, aged 31, of Dublin, husbandman.
WEATHERLEY, Thomas, aged 21, of Kent, edge tool maker.
WETHERELL, S., aged 31, of Lincolnshire, bricklayer.
HANHAM, Thos, aged 21, of London, plaisterer.
TURNER, John, aged 25, of London, cordwainer.
DENEAU, Edward, aged 45, of Eaton, schoolmaster.
HOWARD, John, aged 25, of Surrey, smith.
PALFREMAN, Aron, aged 29, of Bucks, book-keeper.
CARRY, John, aged 24, of Fifeshire, stonemason.
EMMINS, William, aged 27, of Lincoln, husbandman.
SEWELL, Thomas, aged 22, of Westminster, book-keeper.
DRAPER, Thomas, aged 22, of London, silk-dyer.
YOUNG, Samuel, aged 21, of Westminster, cordwainer.
WINGFIELD, William, aged 30, of Berks, husbandman.
HOWARD, William, aged 26, of Worcester, schoolmaster.
HOGGART, Robert, aged 21.
DELLEMORE, Robert, aged 22, of London, brazier.
TAYLOR, Chas., aged 41, of London, bricklayer.
GERMAN, Thos, aged 26, of Ireland, schoolmaster.
BRYANT, Lewis, aged 22, of Bath, plaisterer.
BAGWELL, Robert, aged 23, of Westminster, schoolmaster.
RICE, Willm., aged 26, of Essex, husbandman.
SAUNDERS, John, aged 42, of London, peruke maker.
DEMSAY, James, aged 21, of London, husbandman.
LOW, John, aged 23, of Herts., blacksmith.
WILLIAMS, Thos, aged 30, of London, labourer.
CLARK, Geo., aged 18, of Gloucestershire, stocking-weaver.
PEMBERTON, Edward, aged 30, of Stafford, blacksmith.
REILY, Patrick, aged 25, of Ireland, husbandman.
MAJOR, James, aged 27, of Ireland, butcher.
STAPE, Thos, aged 21, of Somerset, woolcomber.
HOW, Isaac, aged 24, of Suffolk, husbandman.

1773, Dec. 11 to 18.—*cont.*
    SANGSTER, Jno., aged 21, of Reading, carpenter.
    PATTERSON, Jno., aged 22, of Aberdeen, gardner.
    LAMBERT, Jas., aged 21, of Middlesex, gardner.
    ASHER, John, aged 28, of Edinburgh, gardner.
    WHITEHEAD, Jas., aged 27, of Edinburgh, cordwainer.
    McKOIN, Thos, aged 28, of London, schoolmaster.
    MERSSEY, Willm., aged 23, of Bucks, husbandman.
    GUNN, Willm., aged 32, of Sunderland, husbandman.
    WALKER, Bar^w, aged 28, of Bucks, sawyer.
    LAMBERT, Geo., aged 25, of Westminster, cordwainer.
    RICHARDS, Benjn, aged 35, of Deptford, mast-maker.
    ORPWOOD, John, aged 25, of Oxford, joyner.
    MILLER, Rich^d, aged 21, of London, necklace maker.
    THAIRJAMES, Thos, aged 21, of London, book-keeper.
    WESTPHAL, Peter, aged 24, of London, husbandman.
    McDONALD, Terence, aged 30, of London, painter.
    THORNBER, John, aged 35, of London, peruke-maker.
    WATSON, Chas., aged 23, of Surrey, baker.
    EDWARDS, Benjn, aged 22, of Somerset, broadcloth weaver.
    BORDEN, Thos, aged 21, of Nottingham, husbandman.
    ALLISON, W^m, aged 18, of London, labourer.
    TURTLE, Thos, aged 21, of Cambridge, husbandman.
    (Ship "Virginia," to Virginia):
    BOYLE, Willm, aged 26, of Ireland, husbandman.
    McCLOUD, Jno., aged 28, of London, labourer.
    MUIR, Alex^r, aged 21, of Scotland, weaver.
    OGELVIE, Robert, aged 19, of London, husbandman.
    TUDER, John, aged 18, of London, leather dresser.
    OAKELEY, John, aged 19, of London, peruke maker.
    WEATHERFIELD, John, aged 20, of London, blacksmith.
    LEEK, John, aged 17, of Worcester, whitesmith.
    ONWIN, John, aged 17, of Greenwich, baker.
    PEMBERTON, Thos, aged 20, of Chester, bricklayer.
    WELCH, John, aged 31, of Surrey, malster.
    WOOD, Thos, aged 23, of Surrey, schoolmaster.
    STEVENSON, Josh., aged 25, of Westminster, carpenter and joyner.

1773, Dec. 11 to 18.—*cont.*

SMITH, Benjⁿ, aged 24, of Westminster, bricklayer.
YEATES, John, aged 24, of Westminster, weaver.
O'BRIAN, Arch^d, aged 24, of Dublin, butcher.
PARROTT, Benjⁿ, aged 32, of London, carpenter.
GARTH, John, aged 39, of London, sawyer.
PARKER, Willm., aged 22, of Deptford, edge tool maker.
THOMAS, Rich^d, aged 36, of London, haberdasher.
DAWSON, John, aged 22, of Surrey, ostler.
HOWARD, Thos, aged 28, of London, surgeon.
 Elizabeth his wife, aged 23.
FOGG, William, aged 23, of Warwickshire, blacksmith.
KILMAN, Willm, aged 23, of Scotland, blacksmith.
HARRIS, Rich^d, aged 35, of London, gardner.
OCKERSHANSON, Jno., aged 25, of London, baker.
JAMESON, Jas., aged 21, of London, husbandman.
KETLER, Jno. Carl, aged 21, of London, taylor.
CAGAUX, Peter, aged 26, of London, cooper.
CHESAILLER, Alex., aged 21, of London, hatter and painter.
YOUNG, Jno., aged 21, of London, blacksmith.
DANE, George, aged 33, of London, cabinet maker.
CHEAUVANT, Jos., aged 20, of London, gilder.
AUBER, Peter, aged 26, of London, dyer.
CHALLE, Peter, aged 23, of London, blacksmith.
DISBONNE, Chas, aged 30, of London, taylor.
MACQUET, Peter, aged 34, of London, locksmith.
PACH, Beate Lowis, aged 28, of London, farmer.
ASHBURNE, William, aged 28, of London, cutler.
HILL, Thos, aged 35, of Essex, schoolmaster.
CHEVAILLIER, Anto., aged 21, of Westminster, brickmaker.
BURGESS, Willm., aged 34, of London, weaver.
HARRIS, Sarah, aged 21, of London, sempstress.
BRANDES, Henry, aged 33, of London, cordwainer.
ISAAC, Jos., aged 19, of London, peruke maker.
LAWRENCE, Antho., aged 36, of London, cabinet maker.
FLEMMING, Jas., aged 26, of Cornwall, husbandman.
 All the foregoing went as indentured servants for four years.

In the Public Record Office, London.

PORT OF LONDON.

1773, Dec. 18 to 25 (ship "Carolina," to Virginia).
SMITH, Willoughby, aged 19, of Norfolk, carpenter.
DURRED, William, aged 15, of Isle of Ely, husbandman.
FISH, Jos^a, aged 19, of Bristol, bricklayer.
COLE, John, aged 21, of London, carpenter.
WEBB, John, aged 21, of Gloucestershire, husbandman.
SMITH, James, aged 23, of London, book-keeper.
HOLMES, John, aged 32, of London, carpenter.
CAMPION, German, aged 29, of Derby, sawyer.
FULCHER, William, aged 21, of Norwich, carpenter.
GOODLEY, John, aged 23, of Surrey, peruke maker.
CRAIG, George, aged 27, of Middlesex, gardner.
COATS, Henry, aged 37, of Yorkshire, taylor.
WELLETT, Daniel, aged 27, of London, schoolmaster.
BARGET, Thomas, aged 26, of London, taylor.
RAYNELLS, Arthur, aged 23, of Dublin, husbandman.
WRIGHT, John, aged 23, of London, husbandman.
CARTIS, William, aged 25, of London, carpenter.
SPENCE, Henry, aged 25, of London, tallow chandler.
FRY, John, aged 18, of Hants, husbandman.

(Ship "Susanna," to Virginia):
PRICE, Edward, aged 33, of Warwickshire, husbandman.
BOWEN, William, aged 20, of Surrey, bricklayer.
BALDWIN, W^m, aged 22, of London, carpenter.
DENNIS, Richard, aged 24, of Worcester, husbandman.
PARKER, William, aged 25, of Surrey, butcher.
GRIMES, John, aged 25, of London, bricklayer.
ALFRED, Robert, aged 22, of Devonshire, husbandman.
WIGHAM, John, aged 23, of Lancashire, gardener.
WASTENAYS, John, aged 20, of London, bricklayer.
MAYO, Robt, aged 23, of London, carver.
MARSH, Page, aged 28, of London, weaver.
PALRIM, John, aged 21, of London, cabinet maker.
All the foregoing went as indentured servants.

INDEX OF NAMES

INDEX OF NAMES

Abbes, 25
Abley, 42
Abraham, 172
Abram, 106
Adams, 120, 130, 160, 180, 190, 193
Adlington, 116
Ady, 122
Aisbie, 130
Aitken, 92
Akehurst, 144
Akin, 171
Alder, 128
Aldey, 37
Aldous, 119
Aldworth, 41, 118
Alexander, 61, 92
Alfred, 200
Alkyn, 101, 108
All, 188
Allaway, 61
Allcock, 190
Allduck, 190
Allen, 47, 54, 62, 67, 111, 123
Alley, 192
Alleyne, 79
Allin, 20
Allison, 156, 198
Allott, 65
Almond, 134
Alsop, 76
Altham, 13
Alven, 154
Alvey, 36
Amherst, 89
Amies, 152
Amrey, 20

Anderson, 98, 111, 158, 188
Andrews, 2, 8, 20, 33, 114, 115, 120, 123
Angells, 30
Annely, 72
Anscombe, 127
Anthony, 3, 105, 128
Applebee, 176
Arckbold, 189, 193
Archer, 34, 110
Argall, 4
Argyle, 87
Armstrong, 12, 165
Armye, 27, 139
Arnold, 2, 3
Arondell, 5
Arthington, 136
Arthur, 38
Ashburne, 199
Ashby, 101, 102
Ashcom, 54
Asher, 198
Ashurst, 121
Ashley, 86, 102
Aston, 19, 116
Atcheson, 192
Atkins, 26
Atkinson, 1
Auber, 199
Augur, 144
Austin, 16, 33
Avery, 129, 178
Ayray, 60

Babb, 8
Bach, 73
Bachelor, 30, 31

Bagling, 181
Bagwell, 197
Bailey, 79, 185
Baker, 26, 89, 96, 131, 171, 183, 192
Baldwin, 21, 200
Balfour, 92
Ball, 98, 177, 191
Ballyntine, 171
Baltimore, 19, 23
Banester, 159
Banks, 152
Barber, 35, 147
Barclay, 88
Bard, 80
Barget, 200
Barham, 37
Barker, 28, 188
Barlowe, 37
Barmby, 148
Barneham, 101
Barnes, 6, 190
Barnett, 179
Barradaile, 73
Barrett, 175
Barrow, 189
Barry, 70, 131
Bartin, 144
Bartlett, 4, 131, 178
Barton, 38
Baryhard, 28
Basnett, 75
Batch, 71
Bate, 49
Bateman, 189
Bathurst, 59
Batt(s), 12, 25, 153
Bauldine, 136

Baulke, 26
Bauton, 158
Bawdon, 54
Bayard, 76
Bayliss, 77
Bayly, 129, 168
Bazy, 128
Beale, 142
Beard, 28
Beare, 107
Beauchamp, 70
Beckford, 155, 175
Bedok, 75
Becke, 38, 106, 133
Beekers, 184
Beckman, 90
Beeman, 127
Beeston, 193
Beheathland, 24, 142
Belcher, 98
Bell, 188, 193
Bellingham, 43
Bellinghurst, 77
Bemister, 36
Bennett, 16, 37, 76, 102, 116, 117, 125, 128, 186
Bennington, 2
Benson, 38, 191
Bentley, 45, 185
Berkeley, 125
Bernard, 142, 154
Berridge, 120
Berry, 19
Berthon, 181
Besbeech, 17
Bess(e), 87, 185
Best, 17
Bethell, 196
Bethune, 85
Bettsworth, 162
Bicke, 38
Bickerton, 155
Biddlecombe, 154
Bier, 75
Bigg(s), 6, 52

Biles, 165
Billinghurst, 162
Billockes, 139
Bins, 121
Bircham, 111
Bird, 64
Birkenhead, 152
Biron, 26
Bishop, 50, 115, 187
Bispam, 26
Bisson, 158
Blackburn, 96
Blackler, 8
Blackman, 19, 33
Blades, 192
Blair, 84
Blake, 78, 87, 156, 186
Bland, 55
Blighton, 55
Blindall, 160
Blondall, 135
Bl(o)unt, 2, 120
Blyhton, 141
Boles, 19
Bolleme, 182
Bomper, 85
Bond, 38
Boney, 16
Bonner, 38
Bodker, 115
Booth, 65
Borden, 198
Bordley, 184
Boreel, 32
Boroughes, 103
Boucher, 15
Boulter, 23
Boulton, 11
Bourdett, 72
Bourdon, 10
Bowbrick, 135
Bowdoin, 79, 182
Bowen, 200
Bowler, 154
Bowles, 38, 78, 94, 153

Boyd, 93, 190
Boykett, 30
Boyle, 198
Boylston, 172
Boyse, 134
Bozonne, 111
Brace, 52, 193
Brading, 115
Bradley, 71, 73, 176
Braen, 139
Braines, 22
Braithwaite, 180
Brames, 18
Brandes, 199
Branstone, 170
Brasseur, 70
Bratheridge, 33
Bray, 8
Breedon, 174
Brenton, 10, 69, 158
Bressie, 54
Brestbone, 160
Bretland, 123
Brett, 133
Brewer, 14
Brian, 75
Brice, 193
Brick, 167
Bridger, 61
Bridges, 10, 38
Bridgman, 144
Brigden, 17
Brimsmeades, 132
Brinkerhoff, 80
Brocden, 176
Brock, 119, 167
Brome, 106
Brooke(s), 16, 150, 186, 188
Brown(e), 25, 41, 42, 65, 93, 97, 119, 120, 121, 126, 132, 144, 167, 177, 178, 186, 187, 188, 191
Browning, 11
Bruce, 112, 188

Bruff, 189, 191 *bis*
Bruister, 46
Bryant, 197
Bryen, 159
Bubbe, 136
Buck(e), 5, 30, 62, 190
Buckannan, 187
Buckly, 189
Buckner, 127
Buds, 36
Bulkeley, 109
Buller, 152
Bullington, 43
Bullocke, 130
Burbage, 10
Burchfild, 122
Burdet, 144
Burges(s), 5, 8, 11, 119, 199
Burman, 193
Burna, 87
Burnett, 26
Burnham, 159
Burnley, 91
Burr, 160
Burrell, 121
Burrington, 184
Burrow(s), 162, 180
Burstone, 127
Burton, 14, 21, 27, 101
Bushell, 149
Bushrode, 154
Butler, 14, 30, 36, 37, 44, 145
Buttery, 151
Butts, 194
Byrd, 69, 142

Cæsar, 35
Caffinch, 150
Cagaux, 199
Cage, 13
Calder, 188
Caldwall, 190
Cale, 118
Call(e), 30, 31
Calvert, 19, 23
Camcon, 187
Campbell, 77, 86, 87
Camper, 189, 191
Campion, 200
Caney, 82
Cannon, 38, 103
Cant, 150
Canton, 163
Capell, 42
Carey, 53, 137, 159, 160, 175, 179
Carmichael, 121
Carpenter, 38, 39, 60, 166, 176, 193
Carr(e), 79, 80, 84–86, 179
Carrion, 59
Carroll, 54, 168, 186
Carruthers, 68
Carry, 197
Carslake, 190
Carter, 10, 11, 34, 55, 69, 108, 127, 153, 168, 169, 177
Cartis, 200
Cartwright, 5
Carver, 22
Cassaway, 190
Castle, 9
Catcher, 135
Caulfield, 179
Caunte, 137
Cay, 100
Chaddocke, 47
Chaffey, 51
Chalke, 40
Challe, 199
Chalmers, 70, 173
Chamberlaine, 187
Champion, 17
Champneys, 171
Chandler, 133, 146
Chaplaine, 39
Chaplyn, 4

Chapman, 4, 106, 127
Chaterton, 45
Chatfeeld, 32
Chauncy, 49
Cheauvant, 199
Checkley, 61
Cheesman, 51
Chesailler, 199
Chesewright, 4
Cheshire, 68
Chester, 33, 64
Chevaillier, 199
Chew, 186, 188
Chichester, 177
Chicken, 158
Chill, 28
Chorley, 75
Chrouchley, 104
Church, 33
Churchman, 178
Clansey, 191
Clappum, 27
Clark(e), Clerk(e), 15, 20, 44, 52, 81, 144, 146, 155, 189, 197
Clayborne, 9, 34, 153, 182
Claydon, 24
Clayton, 38, 65, 117
Cliff(e), 52
Clifton, 28
Clipsham, 136
Cloak, 192
Clopton, 74
Clow, 100
Coats, 200
Coby, 144
Cochet, 48
Cochroft, 139
Cocke, 139
Cockraine, 192
Coffin, 40
Cokayne, 36
Coke, 26, 158
Colclough, 159
Cole, 13, 17, 74, 200

Coleman, 31, 181
Collet(t), 75, 107
Collier, 135
Collins, 37, 157, 183, 192, 196
Colly, 128
Colthurst, 36
Columbell, 15
Commelin, 80
Compton, 180
Conant, 46
Connerly, 189
Constable, 104
Converse, 115, 149
Cook(e), 39, 130, 143, 177, 190, 192
Cookerill, 167
Coombe, 14, 173
Cooper, 44, 141, 151, 155
Coore, 65
Corbin, 142, 143
Cornocke, 27
Cornwallis, 23, 187
Corwin, 132
Cory, 122
Cosby, 179
Cottington, 19
Cotton, 189
Couchman, 16
Coursey, 186, 189
Cowell, 130
Cowlington, 81
Cox, 56, 58, 172, 187
Coxce, 124
Cradock, 36
Craig, 200
Crake, 108, 155
Cramond, 100
Craven, 67, 89
Crawford, 94
Crawley, 44, 160
Cray, 154
Crayford, 143
Creed, 15
Creeke, 123

Crick, 178
Crisp, 196
Crooke(s), 64, 160
Cropton, 144
Crosse, 162
Crouch, 128
Crow(e), 28, 132
Crumsey, 57
Cugley, 118
Cullen, 193
Culpepper, 24
Cultain, 87
Cuningham, 65
Cunstable, 102
Curnocke, 27
Currie, 183
Curtes, 172
Custis, 64
Cutling, 149
Cutlord, 138
Cutter, 158
Cuyler, 80

Dagger, 143
Dagord, 130
Dale, 4, 32, 75
Danby, 153
Dane, 199
Daniell, 160
Darby, 135
Darnal, 188
Davidson, 192
Davies, 5, 131, 139, 157
Davis, 36, 67, 87, 146
Davye, 7, 146
Dawson, 65, 77, 199
Day, 88, 160, 178
Deane, 160
Dearslye, 106
Delahunty, 192
Delaware, 104
Dellemore, 197
Deloraine, 180
Demsay, 197
Deneau, 197

Denham, 111
Denn(e), 24
Dennis, 200
Dent, 97
Dere, 131
Desmeker, 32
Devenish, 163
Devonport, 150
Dewell, 27
Dewer, 31
De Windt, 77
Dewlittle, 47
Dickson, 78
Diggs, 187
Dillon, 177
Dimonds, 136
Disbonne, 199
Dison, 179, 185
Ditchfield, 68
Dixon, 43, 119
Dobbett, 141
Dobson, 191
Docke, 28
Dolvin, 187
Domelaw, 6
Done, 150
Dorrell, 47
Dorsey, 186
Doubble, 127
Doud, 86
Douglas, 79
Dove, 168
Dover, 162
Doves, 37
Downe(s), 148, 192
Downeman, 4
Doyley, 60
Draiton, 142
Drake, 14, 155
Drant, 128
Draper, 162, 197
Driver, 142
Drury, 151
Dry, 66
Drywood, 156

Duckworth, 148
Duddlestone, 167
Dudley, 22, 39, 61, 123
Duerid, 46
Duke, 37, 53, 91, 136
Dukinfield, 75
Dulany, 186, 188, 189
Dumer, 43
Dun, 128
Dunbar, 86
Dunkin, 17
Dunkley, 59
Dunn, 72
Dunstar, 121
Dunton, 167
Durant, 110
Duron, 174
Durred, 200
Dymond, 75
Dyson, 179

Eades, 136
Earle, 54, 142
Eastwood, 149
Eaton, 31, 35, 50, 127
Eavens, 157
Edgar, 75
Edmondson, 192
Edwards, 15, 69, 110, 114, 132, 150, 192, 198
Eede, 114
Egelden, 17
Eger, 25, 134
Elam, 98
Elbridge, 118
Eldred, 136
Elicott, 140
Elliot, 123, 183
Ellis, 14, 105, 135, 150
Elsey, 127
Elsworth, 91
Eltonhead, 153
Emmins, 197
Emory, 187, 191
Endecott, 22

Ensigne, 48
Erington, 158
Eslake, 24
Evance, 75
Evans, 149, 175, 189, 191, 196
Everard, 46, 194
Everitt, 189
Evers, 86
Ewell, 16
Ewen, 126
Ewes, 130
Eyton, 137

Fadding, 145
Fairman, 160 *bis*
Fairweather, 177
Fallowfield, 192
Farle, 30
Farmer, 96, 126
Farrar, 6, 107, 140
Farrell, 165
Farthinge, 157
Fa(u)ssett, 15
Fawdin, 145
Fawne, 142, 143
Feast, 160
Feilden, 15
Felgate, 15, 19
Fenn, 123
Fenwick, 9, 113, 180, 190
Ferne, 106
Fetters, 189, 193
Fidler, 56
Field, 175, 188
Fifett, 156
Finlayson, 183
Fish, 114 *bis*, 200
Fisher, 114, 132
Fiske, 39
Fitzpen, 135
Flat, 86
Fleming, 93, 162, 192, 199
Fletcher, 24, 84
Fluellinge, 26

Flynton, 105
Fogg, 199
Foll, 76
Ford, 8, 16, 60, 130, 140
Forth, 44
Foster, 68, 190
Foullard, 149
Fox, 98, 149, 174, 196
Foy, 166
Frampton, 189
Frank, 107, 145
Franklin, 85
Fraser, 181
Frazier, 192
Freeman, 22, 62, 63, 148
French, 140
Frere, 144, 147
Frink, 89
Frisby, 142, 143
Frost, 99
Fry, 146, 169, 172, 183, 196, 200
Fryer, 112
Fulcher, 200
Fuller, 149
Furze, 62

Gadsden, 194
Gage, 32
Gaines, 97
Galhie, 181
Gallant, 16
Ganton, 127
Gard(i)ner, 78, 179
Garey, 191
Garnsey, 149
Garretty, 191
Garth, 199
Gascoigne, 178
Gates, 160
Gaudey, 45
Gaward, 147
Geates, 133
Geere, 21, 22
German, 197

Gerrard, 19
Gelley, 193
Gibbes, 75, 180
Gibbins, 113
Gibson, 155, 158
Gifford, 42
Gilberte, 150
Gildart, 65
Giles, 144
Gill, 30
Gillam, 120
Gilles, 92
Gippes, 21
Gladin, 78
Glencross, 59
Godart, 55
Godin, 66, 77
Godwin, 61
Goldsmith, 77
Golightly, 180
Golipher, 128
Gondry, 31
Gooch, 154, 174, 179
Goodall, 136
Goodfellowe, 27
Goodley, 200
Goodman, 168
Goodyere, 128
Goose, 140
Gorges, 49
Gos, 32
Gosnold, 102
Gott, 34
Gough, 147
Gould, 85
Goulder, 25
Goundrey, 12
Gounter, 132
Graby, 124
Graham, 191-2
Granger, 30, 31
Grape, 170
Grason, 187, 189
Grave(s), 12, 37, 54
Gray, 92, 166

Gread, 131
Greeham, 154
Green(e), 19, 21, 22, 55, 73, 106
Greenhill, 90
Gregge, 20
Gregory, 143
Gregson, 35
Grendon, 53
Grennill, 22
Gresley, 97
Grevett, 11
Greville, 185
Grewes, 54
Grible, 131
Grice, 83
Griffin, 80, 85, 172, 188, 190, 191
Griffith, 171
Grigg, 35, 147
Grimes, 200
Grinhill, 131
Gronous, 80
Groome, 50, 140
Groves, 183
Gud, 140
Gulliver, 83
Gunn, 198
Gunton, 63
Gwyn, 41

Haberfield, 164
Hack, 188
Hackett, 57
Haddocke, 122
Hage, 190
Haggett, 79
Haines, 113
Halbert, 68
Hale, 151
Halford, 132
Hall, 9, 30, 65, 153, 158, 187-9
Hallett, 65
Halley, 23

Hallfield, 189
Halsall, 68
Halse, 10
Halsted, 139
Hamilton, 59, 189
Hamlin, 58, 59
Hammerton, 70
Hammon(d), 74, 87
Hamor, 105
Hanbury, 72, 182
Handley, 3
Han(d)son, 33, 68
Hanham, 197
Hannen, 79
Hardie, 52
Harding, 4, 72
Hargrave, 194
Harleston, 94
Harnet, 30
Harri(e)s, 17, 38, 54, 131, 149, 191, 199 *bis*
Harryson, 10, 11, 55, 60, 67, 86, 117, 130, 146
Hart, 28, 144, 157, 160, 189, 194
Hartram, 146
Hartwell, 55, 160
Harvey, 43, 44, 47, 57, 61, 67, 81, 83, 91, 94, 98, 100, 119
Harwar, 154
Harwood, 51, 111, 117
Hase, 32
Haskett, 57
Hastings, 194
Hatch, 16, 143
Hathaway, 39
Hatt, 33
Hattone, 112
Haw, 176
Hawker, 49
Hawkins, 140, 186, 190
Hawley, 23, 103
Hay, 193
Hayes, 95, 110

Hayley, 96
Hayne(s), 26, 108, 175
Hayward, 16
Hazard, 48
Hearle, 185
Heath, 188
Hedger, 162
Hemes, 189
Henley, 195
Henshaw, 155
Herne, 160
Hesilrige, 88
Hester, 180
Hewbanck, 191
Hewett, 65
Hickmas, 175
Higgins, 114, 178, 188, 193
Higginson, 150
Highmore, 83
Higon, 82
Hill, 7, 45, 57, 128, 165, 173, 187, 197, 199
Hilton, 64
Hinckley, 17
Hind, 101
Hipkis, 136
Hitch, 48
Hitchins, 161
Hoare, 145
Hobbs, 170
Hobeme, 144
Hockaday, 117
Hockley, 83
Hodges, 136, 154
Hodiline, 36
Hoggart, 197
Holbrough, 137
Holding, 186
Hollier, 70
Holly, 133
Holm, 93
Holman, 164
Ho(l)mes, 6, 16, 64, 100, 124, 190, 200

Honywood, 24
Hooke, 31, 68
Hooker, 25, 38, 40, 113, 134
Hooton, 79
Hope, 24
Hopkins, 50, 71, 73, 113, 114, 135, 144, 179, 182
Hopkinson, 28
Horder, 128
Hore, 163
Horne, 52
Horton, 77
Hoskins, 34
Hothersall, 144
Houghton, 35
Houlde, 33
Hovell, 36
How, 197
Howard, 176, 186, 197 bis, 199
Howchin, 43
Howell, 186, 193
Hubbard, 145
Huddleston, 120
Hudson, 151
Huett, 113
Huger, 122
Hughes, 189
Hull, 73
Humble, 103 bis
Hume, 80, 171
Humphry, 22
Hunter, 29, 88, 190
Huntley, 38
Hurrell, 70
Hurst, 154
Hutchinson, 26, 77, 79
Hyatt, 190
Hyde, 132

Iles, 78
Impey, 188
Ingland, 30
Inglesby, 109

Ingram, 141, 149
Inman, 79, 88
Irby, 141
Ireland, 107
Isaac, 199
Izard, 87, 171

Jackson, 41, 42
Jacob, 138
James, 29, 115, 148, 153
Jameson, 199
Janson, 124
Jarman, 192
Jarratt, 58
Jarves, 24
Jauneye, 41
Jeakins, 16
Jeffery(s), 69, 96, 159, 191
Jekyll, 81
Jelfe, 193
Jenkins, 30, 72, 179
Jen(n)ings, 16, 102, 147, 184, 193
Jennison, 31
Jenys, 75, 171
Jepson, 31
Jerome, 56
Johnson, 11, 30, 42, 48, 126, 142, 143, 148, 159, 191
Jones, 17, 19, 33, 45, 78, 153, 189-193
Jordaine, 149
Jordan, 36
Joyce, 48
Jubbs, 143

Karmihill, 121
Keado, 125
Keene, 182
Keith, 88, 95, 175
Kelley, 121, 191
Kello, 84
Kellum, 137
Kelway, 137

Kemble, 166, 187
Kemis, 102
Kempe, 28, 117, 125
Kendall, 102, 187, 188
Kennede, 12
Kennett, 167
Kenny, 172
Kent, 115, 120
Kerridge, 129
Ketchrell, 16
Ketler, 199
Kett, 39
Keys, 11
Kighte, 109
Kilby, 73
Killingworth, 158
Kilman, 199
Kilner, 167
King(e), 27, 128, 139
Kingsmill, 7
Kinnersley, 176
Kinnimont, 187
Kirkham, 151, 191
Kirton, 117
Knight, 191
Knock, 189
Knolles, 114
Knott, 32
Knowles, 165, 183
Kyes, 4

Lacy, 20
Lagee, 111
Lahorne, 168
Laing, 70, 173
Lake, 153
Lambe, 104
Lamber, 193
Lambert, 21, 157, 198 *bis*
Lanchester, 94
Landerry, 87
Lane, 8, 55, 60, 64, 80, 137, 164, 191
Lanes, 156
Langley, 13, 63, 101

Langrish, 154
Langworth, 24
Lapham, 16
Larkes, 169
Larkin, 160
Latham, 121
Lathbury, 151
Launder, 22
Laurence, 111, 199
Laverton, 191
Lavington, 37
Lawndey, 160
Lawne, 105
Lawry, 177
Lawson, 130
Leach, 35, 176
Leadbetter, 109
Leaming, 108
Leamy, 100
Le Clerc, 181
Lee, 34, 63, 99, 125, 135, 149, 161, 191
Leech, 26, 65
Leek, 198
Legoe, 181
Leicester, 13
Leigh, 34, 68, 73, 131
Leister, 101
Lench, 35
Lendrum, 98
Leonards, 23
Lewes, 36, 114
Lewin, 31
Lewis, 17, 26, 54, 69, 128, 171
Linsford, 155
Lisney, 106
Lister, 115, 116, 139
Littlepage, 91
Livingston, 80
Lloyd, 33, 66, 67, 79, 157, 171, 187
Lock(e), 28, 56, 156
Logan, 97
Long, 174

Loockerman, 187
Loton, 142
Love, 17, 133, 156
Low(e), 11, 58, 193, 197
Lowfield, 149
Lowry, 74
Lowther, 8
Lucas, 40, 50, 160
Lucke, 122, 147
Ludlowe, 150 *bis*, 154
Lunsford, 125
Luscombe, 70
Lux, 54
Lymburner, 95
Lynch, 186
Lyne(s), 37, 168
Lyon, 192

McAll, 183
McCloud, 198
McColl, 93
Maccubbins, 186
McDonald, 198
McKey, 77
Mackintosh, 76
McKoin, 198
Macocke, 105
Macqvet, 199
Major, 37, 197
Makepeace, 132
Malbone, 183
Man(n)ing(e), 80, 127, 138
Mansell, 189
Mansfield, 157, 193
March, 63
Marcombe, 27
Markland, 28
Marriner, 153
Mars, 87
Marsh, 71, 73, 200
Marshall, 150, 160
Marter, 162
Martin(e), 10, 29, 40, 102, 143, 150, 157, 177
Martindale, 68

Mason, 17, 21, 26, 35, 45, 46, 113, 153
Mathews, 6, 69, 106, 142
Matts, 157
Mawson, 164
Maxwell, 184
May, 127, 130, 141
Mayes, 87
Maynard, 110
Mayo, 200
Mead, 166
Meadows, 45, 93
Mechell, 140
Mekin, 106
Mellowes, 132
Melville, 188
Menefie, 115
Meredith, 147
Mereweather, 91
Merriday, 193
Merriman, 156
Merssey, 198
Messe, 160
Messenger, 78
Messer, 185
Mico, 84
Middleton, 8, 107
Miller, 54, 187, 190, 192, 198
Mill(e)s, 62, 74, 112, 130, 162
Millington, 190
Millowes, 163
Milwarde, 5
Ming(e), 55, 61
Minifee, 19
Minifrey, 29
Minshull, 153
Minskie, 187
Mitchell, 177
Modyford, 78
Mojar, 128
Molineux, 104, 193
Molley, 77
Mones, 28

Monger, 162
Monser, 119
Monson, 153
Montague, 131, 137
Moody, 88, 95, 175
Mooncke, 22
Moore, 21, 43, 65, 96, 118, 191
Moors, 192
Mordant, 9
Morden, 45
More, 84
Morecroft, 33
Moretan, 128
Morgan, 45, 58, 197
Morley, 180
Morrison, 95
Morth, 26
Mortimore, 191
Morton, 20, 112, 159
Moss, 74
Mostyn, 171
Moult, 120
Moultrie, 171
Moye, 47
Muir, 93, 198
Muleston, 12
Mullard, 148
Munday, 120, 123
Munro, 196
Murdock, 98, 177
Murphey, 191 *bis*
Murray, 54, 178, 192
Murrell, 142, 143
Myers, 175
Myns, 37

Nant, 28
Nason, 63
Naylor, 128
Neale, 186, 187
Nelson, 3, 43
Nethersole, 18
Neuley, 17
Nevaros, 67

Nevinson, 162
Newarke, 106
Newbury, 62
Newell, 192
Newland, 136
Newman, 27, 150
Newport, 102
Newsom, 177
Newton, 54
Nicholson, 88, 142, 171, 189
Nicklis, 124
Nickolls, 119, 132
Nightingale, 117
Noble, 126
Noke, 128
Norcott, 30
Norcross, 47
Norman(s), 8, 156
Norris, 39
North, 145
Northens, 43
Norton, 35, 43, 108
Nott, 8
Nottingham, 167
Noyes, 46, 87
Numan, 120
Nurry, 140
Nuse, 5
Nye, 22, 110

Oakley, 67, 72, 198
Oales, 158
O'Brian, 199
Ockershanson, 199
Odingsells, 26
Offspring, 38
Oge, 4
Ogilvie, 84, 93, 96, 198
Olave, 185
Olbolston, 117
Oldfield, 65
Oldson, 191
Oliver, 50, 85, 132
Olliffe, 105

— 211 —

Onwin, 198
Ormston, 88
Orpwood, 183, 198
Osborne, 4, 62
Osler, 75
Osmond, 187
Oswald, 173
Ovell, 31
Overinge, 155
Overton, 61
Oxenden, 128
Oxwick, 116

Pach, 199
Pacheury, 17
Page, 19, 30, 66
Paguy, 184
Pain, 61
Painter, 187
Pale, 147
Palfreman, 197
Palinge, 32
Palmer, 31, 145
Palrim, 200
Pankhurst, 22
Papworth, 106
Pardie, 44
Parke, 15, 55, 58, 64, 65, 164
Parker, 69, 76, 124, 127, 129, 151, 159, 163, 186, 199, 200
Parkin, 160
Parkinson, 124
Parks, 44
Parrott, 199
Parry, 29, 99
Parsyvall, 137
Paske, 148
Patterson, 192, 198
Paule, 147
Pavier, 103
Pawlett, 6
Payne, 118
Peacocke, 120
Peake, 165

Pe(a)rsehouse, 71, 73
Pearson, 65, 189
Peart, 136, 151
Peaseley, 19
Peate, 20, 190
Pecke, 45
Peerce, 31
Peers, 4
Peirsey, 9
Pell, 82
Pemberton, 38, 197, 198
Pendle, 29
Peney, 57
Pen(ne), 24, 60, 153
Pennington, 13, 34, 38
Pennoyer, 36, 37
Penny, 40
Penros, 135
Pensax, 52
Pepys, 9
Perce, 37
Percivall, 1
Percy, 149
Perien, 16
Perkins, 114
Perks, 44
Perry, 10, 11, 45, 53, 55–68, 71–76, 90, 95, 100, 115, 164
Perryor, 15
Persey, 7
Peter(s), 22, 39, 126
Phillips, 56, 147, 149
Philpot, 195
Phippen, 120, 135
Phipps, 161
Phyn, 97
Pickering, 63
Pickett, 142, 160, 188
Pierce, 150, 180
Piggott, 126
Pilgrim, 82
Pinckney, 75
Pinner, 157
Pitchforke, 111

Pitt, 164
Plaisted, 82
Plampin, 44
Playter, 72
Plowden, 153
Plowman, 191
Pomeroy, 183
Pontis, 5
Poole, 65
Pooley, 7
Pope, 30, 175
Popham, 54
Pore, 57
Porter, 187
Portman, 131
Potley, 104
Pott, 11
Potter, 25, 54
Potts, 75
Povey, 55
Powell, 104, 123
Powle, 105
Pratt, 190
Prentis, 182
Presson, 143
Preston, 31
Price, 116, 150, 175, 186, 189, 190, 200
Pringle, 89, 180
Prioleau, 171
Probart, 80
Procter, 4
Proud, 54
Proute, 192
Pryor, 117, 160
Pugh, 192
Purnell, 122
Pyers, 5
Pyner, 157

Quayle, 98
Quincy, 79

Rabasha, 39
Raglass, 189

Rainscroft, 27
Rainsdon, 83
Rake, 183
Ramsaye, 26
Randall, 133
Randolph, 182
Ransfield, 191
Ratcliffe, 1, 102
Rawlings, 149
Ray, 190
Rayment, 12, 139
Reade(e), 142, 155, 158, 185
Redman, 20
Reed, 86, 158, 179
Reeley, 136
Reeves, 28
Reid, 92
Reily, 197
Remnant, 38
Reston, 18
Rey, 15
Reynells, 200
Ribot, 181
Rice, 192, 197
Rich, 57
Richards, 16, 54, 58, 142, 143, 198
Richardson, 4, 30, 94, 170
Richbell, 111
Rickards, 69
Riddle, 190
Ring(e), 26
Risby, 38
Risle, 121
Roberts, 72, 79, 136
Robertson, 77, 92, 93
Robins, 139
Robinson, 189
Robinson-Austen, 16
Roche, 145
Rock, 190
Rogers, 37, 43, 114, 160
Rolffe, 5

Rollinson, 145
Rootes, 17
Roper, 137
Rose, 6, 117
Rosier, 139
Ross, 195
Rousby, 188
Rowe, 10
Rowland, 187, 188
Rowlston, 13
Rowney, 193
Royden, 128, 157
Rudyard, 152
Ruhlee, 125
Russell, 7, 22, 42, 90, 94, 105, 159, 171
Rutledge, 75, 180
Ryan, 182, 192
Ryley, 116

Sadler, 155, 170
Sale, 170
Sammes, 29
Sancarfe, 53
Sandall, 120
Sanders, 127, 160
Sanderson, 157
Sandes, 23
Sandford, 169
Sandwell, 169
Sandys, 107
Sangster, 198
Sapsford, 56
Sarly, 85
Satterfield, 190
Saunders, 23, 197
Savage, 74, 78, 90
Sawyer, 36
Sayers, 17, 157
Scatchell, 43
Schapes, 139
Schubert, 83
Schuyler, 80
Scollay, 85

Scott, 51, 56, 71, 93, 9, 148, 152, 173, 180, 192
Screven, 94
Seares, 178
Searle, 46
Sedgwick, 73
Seele, 165
Seemer, 139
Selleck, 59
Seth, 186
Seton, 183
Seward, 137
Sewell, 197
Seymour, 190, 191
Shakespeare, 114
Shapton, 131
Sharpe, 6, 153
Sharpham, 147
Sharples, 73
Shawe, 39, 106, 156
Shed, 176
Shedden, 95
Shehane, 189
Shemand, 26
Shepherd, 107, 127, 136, 176
Sherbrooke, 95
Sherley, 28, 104
Sherman, 65, 196
Sherrard, 65, 153
Sherver, 87
Sherwood, 3, 90, 164, 173, 188
Shipp, 157
Shurt, 46
Sicklemore, 1
Silton, 98
Simmory, 109
Simon, 195
Sinclair, 79, 192
Sivier, 101
Skinner, 74, 193
Slaughter, 192
Smallay, 4
Smart, 115, 177

Smease, 120
Smith, 7, 19, 31, 78, 86, 94, 99, 102, 105, 111, 113, 114, 119, 120, 123, 128, 130, 132, 138, 141, 153, 155, 162, 166, 169, 181, 184, 186, 192 bis, 197, 198, 200 bis
Smythson, 7
Snoud, 177
Snow, 137
Sole, 28, 39
Solomon, 127
Somers, 1
Southerne, 12
Sowter, 82
Spackman, 27
Sparhawke, 129
Sparke, 149
Sparrow, 61, 185
Spelman, 10
Spence, 200
Spencer, 89
Spice, 30
Spillard, 140
Sprigg, 123
Spurdance, 138
Spurr, 120
Sputledge, 77
Stagg, 42
Stallinge, 33
Stape, 197
Staples, 78
Starre(e), 17, 30
Stawell, 168
Stead, 194
Stedman, 130, 159
Steele, 32
Steers, 171
Stegge, 141
Stent, 160
Stephens, 137, 168
Stert, 40
Stevens, 40, 126, 128, 129, 147, 168

Stevenson, 194, 198
Stockdale, 66
Stocker, 185
Stocks, 101
Stockton, 5
Stoddard, 77
Stolion, 110
Stome, 12
Stone, 15, 29, 113, 142, 143, 178
Stopgate, 40
Storey, 190
Strabridge, 131
Streeting, 40
Strettle, 176
Stretton, 25
Stroud, 25
Stubbs, 179
Sullivant, 188
Summers, 68, 99
Sumner, 170
Sutton, 16, 17, 151, 190, 191
Swain, 172
Swan(n), 28, 150
Sweat, 193
Sweeting, 160
Swyer, 19
Symes, 11
Symon(d)s, 10, 111
Syms, 39

Taberer, 145
Tab(u)ry, 54, 87
Tanner, 193
Tapp, 35
Taylor, 30, 38, 69, 127, 187, 189, 190, 197
Templeman, 195
Terrett, 53
Thairjames, 198
Theaton, 158
Thew, 156
Thomas, 69, 102, 155, 160, 171, 188 bis, 199

Thom(p)son, 11, 33, 89, 96, 104, 191
Thomsin, 13
Thornber, 198
Thorne, 38
Thornebush, 140
Thoro(w)good, 15, 83, 160, 171
Thorpe, 123
Thurmer, 33
Tice, 128
Tielroos, 32
Tilden, 16
Tilghman, 186
Todd, 25
Topper, 22
Topping, 48
Torkington, 144
Towers, 195
Townes, 99
Toy, 87
Tracy, 62
Traherne, 50, 160
Trent, 183
Trecothick, 81
Trerise, 41
Trevethan, 83
Trott, 154
Tucker, 10, 177
Tuder, 163, 198
Tuesly, 22
Tufton, 21
Tuite, 65, 189, 193
Tully, 190
Turgis, 156
Turkey, 17
Turner, 110, 176, 197
Turtle, 198
Turton, 159
Turway, 20
Tyas, 97
Tyler, 119

Underhill, 130, 134
Underwood, 18, 82, 114

Ungle, 187
Uptone, 11

Vage, 120
Vallette, 80
Vaningbro, 68
Vardill, 85
Varonne, 127
Varvell, 116
Vassall, 52
Vaughan, 19, 82
Venables, 152
Veren, 46
Vernald, 142
Vincent, 178
Viner, 150
Vivian, 132
Voyley, 24

Wadham, 175
Wakefield, 64
Waldron, 154
Walford, 132
Walker, 27, 30, 38, 53, 63,
 99, 124, 130, 138, 158,
 171, 179, 190, 198
Wall, 76, 140
Wallace, 68, 188
Wallis, 5, 128
Walter(s), 147, 189
Walton, 130
Wandley, 132
Wane, 11
Ward, 9, 14, 15, 26, 193
Warden, 181
Wareing, 171
Warner, 12, 86, 109, 154
Warnett, 11, 12
Warren, 138
Warrham, 113
Washborne, 38
Wastenays, 200
Waters, 13, 64
Waterson, 170
Watkin, 18

Watson, 121, 145, 157,
 158, 198
Watt(s), 24, 71, 77, 80,
 189
Weatherfield, 198
Weatherley, 197
Webb, 33, 36, 45, 120, 200
Webber, 148
Webster, 113, 154, 192
Weeden, 136, 191
Weeks, 66
Welch, 184, 198
Wellett, 200
Wells, 17, 19, 38, 113, 163
Welson, 141
Wendell, 79
Wentworth, 79, 85, 86
West, 2, 6, 7, 105, 161
Westhorpe, 127, 155
Westphal, 198
Wetherell, 197
Whaley, 193
Whaplett, 20
Wharton, 59
Whatton, 62
Wheatley, 31
Wheeler, 38, 47, 188
Whetcombe, 42
Whitbye, 122
White, 10, 26, 105, 116,
 154, 158, 174
Whitehead, 114, 198
Whiteside, 65
Whitfield, 86
Whithorne, 101
Whitman, 139
Whitney, 103
Whittacre, 148
Whittenbury, 160
Whittington, 180
Whitworth, 163
Whytting, 113
Wicks, 161
Wigham, 200
Wilcocks, 34, 66

Wilcox, 5, 44
Wild, 123
Wilkes, 18, 175
Wilkins, 167
Wilkinson, 12, 99, 187
Willen, 193
William(s), 94, 131, 140,
 143, 148, 164, 197
Williamson, 51, 52, 117,
 158
Willis, 67, 75, 105, 113
Wills, 71
Willshire, 79
Wilson, 22, 54, 68, 108,
 128, 138, 150, 190, 193
Windus, 91, 122
Wingfield, 102, 197
Winstanley, 94
Winter, 147
Winthrop, 22
Wintower, 147
Wise, 16, 63, 169
Wiseman, 127
Witham, 43, 160
Witherell, 16
Witheridge, 8
Witherley, 16
Wittes, 101
Woff, 179
Wollaston, 21
Wollestone, 160
Wood(s), 25, 134, 184, 198
Woodbridge, 79, 129
Woodcock, 34
Wooderife, 142
Woodward(e), 6, 112
Woolf, 102
Woolgar, 180
Woolno, 43
Wooters, 191
Worcester, 33, 44
Worey, 42
Wormehill, 43
Wormeley, 125
Wotton, 147

Wraxhall, 12
Wright, 59, 83, 93, 200
Wrightson, 190 *bis*
Wyatt, 62
Wyche, 107

Yardley, 9

Yarway, 111
Yarworth, 34
Yeamans, 77
Yeardley, 5, 9
Yeates, 199
Yeomans, 137, 172
Yewell, 192 *bis*

Young, 128, 142, 143, 174, 184, 192, 197, 199
Younges, 119
Yslebee, 32

Zealee, 139
Zouch, 26

www.ingramcontent.com/pod-product-compliance
Lightning Source LLC
Chambersburg PA
CBHW050145170426
43197CB00011B/1967